A Fresh Twist on
FABRIC FOLDING

❋ 6 TECHNIQUES ❋ 20 QUILT & DÉCOR PROJECTS

Rebecca Wat

C&T PUBLISHING

Text © 2006 Rebecca Wat

Artwork © 2006 C&T Publishing, Inc.

Publisher: Amy Marson

Editorial Director: Gailen Runge

Acquisitions Editor: Jan Grigsby

Editor: Lynn Koolish

Technical Editors: Rene Steinpress, Carolyn Aune, Robyn Gronning

Copyeditor/Proofreader: Wordfirm, Inc.

Design Director/Cover & Book Designer: Christina D. Jarumay

Illustrator: Tim Manibusan

Production Assistant: Tim Manibusan

Photography: Luke Mulks unless otherwise noted

Published by C&T Publishing, Inc., P.O. Box 1456, Lafayette, CA 94549

Library of congress Cataloging-in-Publication Data

Wat, Rebecca,

   A fresh twist on fabric folding : 6 techniques—20 quilt & décor projects / Rebecca Fung Wat.

   p. cm.

Includes index.

ISBN 1-57120-320-6 (paper trade)

1. Patchwork—Patterns. 2. Quilting—Patterns. 3. Origami. I. Title.

TT835.W3753 2006

746.46—dc22

                    2005016368

Printed in China

10 9 8 7 6 5 4 3 2 1

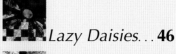

Dedication

To my daughter, Victoria, who is a natural quilt lover

Acknowledgments

Special thanks to:
All the quilters who have written to me—your letters mean a lot.

Denise Fabel, Julie Murphy, and Virginia Dunlop—your exceptional quilting has graced many of my quilts and is a source of inspiration to me.

Lynn Koolish, my wonderful editor—your professionalism as an editor and encouragement as a friend helped move me on.

Everyone at C&T Publishing—you have given me many opportunities; it is my privilege and joy to work with you.

My family here and my parents in Hong Kong—I am forever indebted to you for your love and support.

And most of all, Almighty God, who is my refuge and strength, an ever-present help in trouble.

Introduction

I am a different kind of quilter. I have an acute interest in fabric manipulation and origami. When struck by an inner urge to create something, I just pick up a piece of square fabric or paper and experiment with folding it in different ways. Over the years, with some patience and luck, I have created many extraordinary three-dimensional fabric models, such as flowers, butterflies, stars, pinwheels, bow ties, kimonos, and so on—all fashioned from a single piece of fabric. Most of these models are designed to be pieced into a quilt like regular quilt blocks.

The twenty projects presented here demonstrate how to use these three-dimensional fabric models in quilts. They also display a variety of styles, from traditional to contemporary, occidental to oriental, and a happy marriage of both. You will see adaptations of traditional blocks like Log Cabin and Bow Tie, as well as brand-new ideas that do not conform to any block designs

and are not bound by any rules. Inspired by the way many oriental artworks are mounted, I have made a few quilts with large borders. Not only are these quilts stylish, but they can be easily adjusted to any size as well. I have also found it fascinating to mix and match different fabrics (silk, lace, satin, cotton) with contrasting themes (denim look-alike, oriental floral). In addition, I use a variety of binding methods—straight grain, prairie points, scallops—to give these quilts just the right finishing touch.

I see quilting as a means of self-expression, a way to fulfill the creative urge. If you feel the same way, do not be afraid to try new techniques and explore new avenues. There are always possibilities that we have never realized or taken advantage of. I hope this book will help you see new possibilities, so the next time you pick up a piece of fabric, you will look at it quite differently than before.

Happy quilting!

Getting Started

Each chapter in this book begins by introducing a fabric-folding technique. The folding instructions are provided, followed by several related projects. You will learn six different folding techniques. Then you'll discover how to use these techniques to create fabulous quilts (and some other projects) with dimension and unique texture. You will also learn how to modify or enhance these techniques—pressing them differently, inserting contrasting fabrics, adding embellishments, stuffing them with batting, and so on—which gives you even more options when incorporating them into your projects. The last chapter provides some quilting basics, which beginning quilters will find particularly useful.

One way to make the most out of this book is to learn as many of the folding techniques as possible. You just need to follow the folding instructions in each chapter and practice with scrap fabric or paper. This practice will give you a feel for the time and skill level it takes for each project. Once you have learned to make these fabric models, you will be equipped with new techniques that you can freely apply to many sewing projects.

WORKING ON A PROJECT

- Learn the required folding techniques for the project first.

- Practice the folding techniques on fabrics that will show the finger-pressed creases well. Audition a few different fabrics to be certain you are learning on fabrics with clearly visible creases. Light-colored fabrics usually work well.

- Paper works well for practicing all the techniques except Bow Ties and Pleats, for which stitching is required.

- Follow the folding instructions closely—be sure to read the text *and* look at the accompanying photographs.

- *Finger-press* means to press firmly with your thumbnail.

- *Iron-press* means to press with a steam iron using only an up-and-down motion. You will need to iron-press to set the folds.

- Use pins as needed to help fold or sew the folded blocks together.

- Sew all seams with a $1/4$″ seam allowance.

- Work by the batch whenever possible.

- Your skill and speed will improve tremendously as you progress with a project.

CHOOSING FABRICS

- Choose fabrics that hold creases well. Cotton is the easiest fabric to work with because it tends to hold creases well.

- Silk fabrics usually need to be pressed with a pressing cloth.

- Fabrics that are not prewashed are easier to work with because they have more body than those that have been washed.

- Wash these three-dimensional quilts exactly as you would wash any other quilt. The fabrics you use to make a quilt will determine whether you should dry-clean, hand wash, or machine wash it. If you plan to machine wash these quilts and do not want to repress the folds after washing, tack down the folds.

- Estimated yardage for projects is based on 40″-wide fabrics.

Inside-out Flowers and Variation

The Inside-out Flower is one of the most exciting fabric origami designs I have created. Thanks to its three-dimensional folded petals, this design has an elegant, sophisticated, and truly one-of-a-kind look. Each flower is a simple origami block made from a single square of fabric.

Try out the folding instructions in this chapter. You'll soon see how easily a folded flower can be made and how it can be pieced—the same way you would piece a fabric square—to form a quilt top.

Once you have successfully made the original version of the Inside-out Flower, you are ready to try out some variations. For example, instead of tacking down the center of the flower, insert a piece of contrasting fabric —cotton, silk, lace, or whatever beautiful material you can find—into the flower (refer to Folding Instructions Step 9). Experimenting with combinations of different materials and contrasting prints can often yield surprising, fabulous results. Note that you can use the original Inside-out Flower and its variation inter-changeably in any project. You may choose to do either version or mix and match them. Isn't that fascinating and fun?

FOLDING INSTRUCTIONS

1. Place the fabric wrong side up and fold the square in half. Finger-press. Repeat in the opposite direction to form an intersection of creases.

2. With the fabric wrong side up, bring up a corner to meet the intersection. Finger-press.

3. Repeat Step 2 on the remaining 3 corners.

4. Turn over the fabric. Bring up the bottom edge to align with the intersection. Finger-press and unfold.

5. Repeat Step 4 on the remaining 3 sides to form a square in the center.

6. Use the creases of the square as a reference to bring 2 adjacent edges to the center, creating an ear between them. Finger-press.

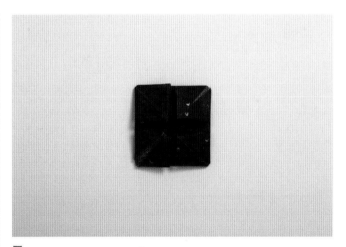

7. Repeat Step 6 on the remaining 3 corners.

8. Gently unfold the 4 side triangles, bringing them from the back to the front. Iron-press to set the folds. You can now piece this as a quilt block.

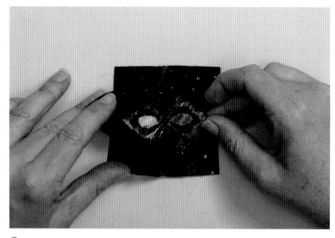

9. For variation, place a piece of lace or contrasting fabric inside the flower.

10. Piece the flower as a quilt block, then turn out the petals.

11. Stitch the petals in place, turning under a little bit of fabric at the tips of the petals

FLOWERS IN A CHESSBOARD

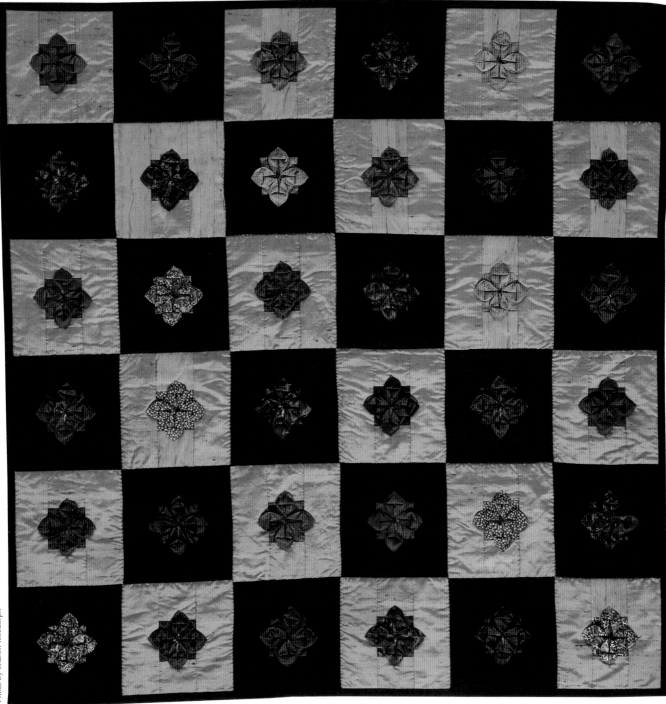

Photo by Sharon Risedorph

Flowers in a Chessboard, 45″ × 45″, block size: 7¹/₂″ × 7¹/₂″, Rebecca Wat

A while ago, I learned from interior design magazines about the concept of minimalism and the power of a simple color scheme. In an attempt to apply that concept—and, quite frankly, to save time—I created this black, gray, and red quilt. The result is not as minimal as what minimalism implies, but it is simple, bold, and elegant.

MATERIALS

Flowers

Flowers ¼ yard each of 6 or more fabrics

Lace ⅛ yard for flower centers

Background 1¼ yards each of a light and a dark fabric

Backing 2¾ yards

Binding 1½ yards for lengthwise cut **OR** ⅝ yard for crosswise cut

Batting 49″ × 49″

CUTTING

Flowers Cut 36 squares 6″ × 6″.

Lace Cut 36 squares 2″ × 2″.

Background

Light fabric

Cut 36 rectangles 3″ × 8″.

Cut 36 squares 3″ × 3″.

Dark fabric

Cut 36 rectangles 3″ × 8″.

Cut 36 squares 3″ × 3″.

Binding Cut strips 3¼″ wide lengthwise or crosswise to total 192″ after piecing the strips end to end (refer to pages 72–74).

FOLDING

Follow the Folding Instructions (**pages 8–10**) to fold the 6″ squares into 36 flowers. Each folded square should measure 3″ × 3″. Insert the 2″ lace squares into the centers of the folded flowers. You do not need to tack down the center squares, because their corners will be caught in the seams that you will sew later.

CONSTRUCTION

1. For each dark or light block, sew a 3″ square to opposite sides of the folded flower, then sew a 3″ × 8″ rectangle to each remaining side. Press.

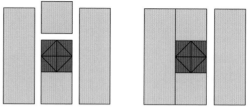

Block Construction

2. Open the petals. Turn under the tips of the petals and stitch them in place (see Step 11, page 10).

3. Arrange all the dark and light blocks as shown in the quilt photo and sew them into rows.

4. Press the seam allowance of each row in alternate directions to make matching the seams easier. Sew the rows together.

5. Refer to pages 69–74 for quilting and finishing.

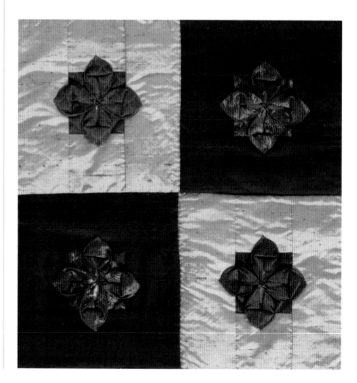

Blue Sapphire I, 85″ × 85″, **block size: 8¹/₂″ × 8¹/₂″**, **Rebecca Wat**

Photo by Sharon Risedorph

*I*f you like the traditional Log Cabin block, you'll love this new version. Replace the center square of the block with an Inside-out Flower to add contrast and soften the boxy logs. The result—a more sophisticated-looking block.

Try arranging these blocks in different ways, just like you would traditional Log Cabin blocks. You will be amazed by all the beautiful patterns you can create. A gemlike quilt such as *Blue Sapphire I* is just one example of what you can do.

MATERIALS

Fabric suggestions 1 fabric for all the folded flowers; 6 lighter-color fabrics and 6 darker-color fabrics for the Log Cabin blocks.

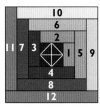

Log Cabin Block

	TWIN	DOUBLE	QUEEN	KING
Finished sizes	68″ × 85″	85″ × 85″	85″ × 93 1/2″	102″ × 102″
Setting	8 × 10	10 × 10	10 × 11	12 × 12
Total blocks	80	100	110	144
Flowers	2 1/2 yards	3 yards	3 1/2 yards	4 1/4 yards
Flower centers	3/8 yard	1/2 yard	1/2 yard	1/2 yard
ALL OTHER PIECES LIGHT FABRICS				
Fabric 1	3/8 yard	1/2 yard	1/2 yard	5/8 yard
Fabric 2	1/2 yard	1/2 yard	1/2 yard	5/8 yard
Fabric 5	1/2 yard	5/8 yard	3/4 yard	7/8 yard
Fabric 6	3/4 yard	7/8 yard	1 yard	1 1/4 yards
Fabric 9	3/4 yard	7/8 yard	1 yard	1 3/8 yards
Fabric 10	3/4 yard	7/8 yard	1 yard	1 3/8 yards
DARK FABRICS				
Fabric 3	1/2 yard	1/2 yard	1/2 yard	5/8 yard
Fabric 4	1/2 yard	5/8 yard	3/4 yard	7/8 yard
Fabric 7	3/4 yard	7/8 yard	1 yard	1 1/4 yards
Fabric 8	3/4 yard	7/8 yard	1 yard	1 3/8 yards
Fabric 11	3/4 yard	7/8 yard	1 yard	1 3/8 yards
Fabric 12	1 yard	1 1/8 yards	1 1/4 yards	1 5/8 yards
Backing	5 yards	7 1/2 yards	7 1/2 yards	9 yards
Binding (crosswise cut)	7/8 yard	1 yard	1 1/8 yards	1 1/4 yards
Batting	72″ × 89″	89″ × 89″	89″ × 98″	106″ × 106″

CUTTING

The following table lists the number of strips to cut and the size to cut each piece from the strips. To use the chart, find the number of pieces you need for the size quilt you are making, then look down the column to see how many strips you need to cut from each fabric.

Note: All Strips are cut crosswise.

As an alternative, you can use the Quick Cutting and Assembly Method (page 15) rather than cutting each piece to size.

	TWIN	DOUBLE	QUEEN	KING
Number of blocks	80	100	110	144
Flowers (cut size: 6″ × 6″) # of 6″ strips	14	17	19	24
Flower centers (cut size: 2″ × 2″) # of 2″ strips	4	5	6	8
ALL OTHER PIECES LIGHT FABRICS				
Fabric 1 (cut size: 1 1/2″ × 3″) # of 1 1/2″ strips	7	8	9	12
Fabric 2 (cut size: 1 1/2″ × 4″) # of 1 1/2″ strips	8	10	11	15
Fabric 5 (cut size: 1 1/2″ × 5″) # of 1 1/2″ strips	10	13	14	18
Fabric 6 (cut size: 1 1/2″ × 6″) # of 1 1/2″ strips	14	17	19	24
Fabric 9 (cut size: 1 1/2″ × 7″) # of 1 1/2″ strips	16	20	22	29
Fabric 10 (cut size: 1 1/2″ × 8″) # of 1 1/2″ strips	16	20	22	29
DARK FABRICS				
Fabric 3 (cut size: 1 1/2″ × 4″) # of 1 1/2″ strips	8	10	11	15
Fabric 4 (cut size: 1 1/2″ × 5″) # of 1 1/2″ strips	10	13	14	18
Fabric 7 (cut size: 1 1/2″ × 6″) # of 1 1/2″ strips	14	17	19	24
Fabric 8 (cut size: 1 1/2″ × 7″) # of 1 1/2″ strips	16	20	22	29
Fabric 11 (cut size: 1 1/2″ × 8″) # of 1 1/2″ strips	16	20	22	29
Fabric 12 (cut size: 1 1/2″ × 9″) # of 1 1/2″ strips	20	25	28	36

Binding Cut strips 3¼″ lengthwise or crosswise to total 318″ for twin, 352″ for double, 369″ for queen, or 420″ for king. Measure to length after piecing strips end to end.

FOLDING

Follow the Folding Instructions (pages 8–10) to fold the 6″ squares into flowers (refer to the chart on the previous page for the number of flowers). Each folded square should measure 3″ × 3″. Insert the 2″ squares into the centers of the folded flowers. You do not need to tack down the center squares, because their corners will be caught in the seams that you will sew later.

CONSTRUCTION

1. For each Log Cabin block, sew the 1½″-wide strips to the center block in the order shown.

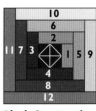

Block Construction

⊞ *Quick Cutting and Assembly Method*
Cut Fabrics 1–12 into 1½″ strips from selvage to selvage. Sew the folded center squares to the Fabric 1 strip, butting the units together, then cut apart the blocks. Rotate the units clockwise and add the Fabric 2 strip in the same way. Repeat with Fabrics 3–12, adding each successive strip.

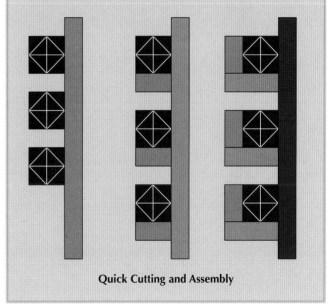

Quick Cutting and Assembly

2. Open the petals. Turn under the tips of the petals and stitch them in place (see Step 11, page 10).

3. Arrange the blocks as shown in the quilt photo. Be sure to double-check each block's orientation.

4. Sew the blocks together by row or section.

5. Refer to pages 69–74 for quilting and finishing.

GLORIOUS BLOSSOMS

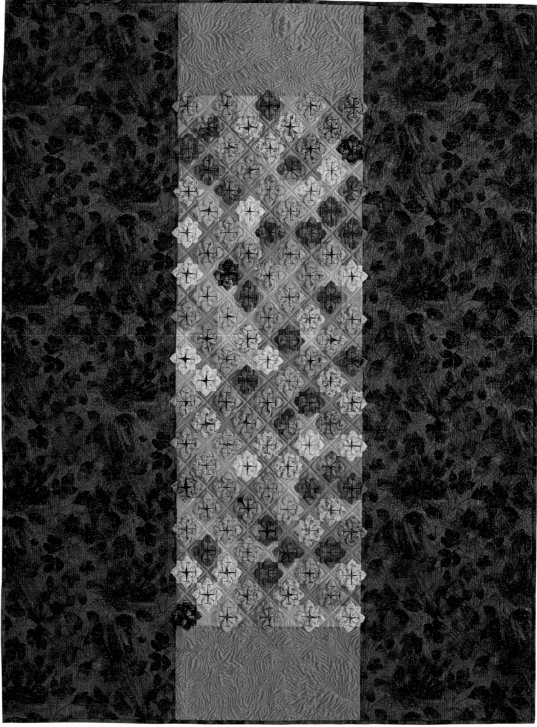

Photo by Sharon Risedorph

Glorious Blossoms, 65″ × 85″, block size: 2$\frac{1}{2}$″ × 2$\frac{1}{2}$″, Rebecca Wat, quilted by Denise Fabel

I sn't this dramatic? This quilt is about contrasts and surprises: a center panel of beautiful, blooming flowers with huge single-fabric borders on both sides. It's a contrast of rich colors and texture against a flat, unified background. Hang this quilt on a tall, empty wall, or use it to cover your bed or dining table. This will surely be a conversation piece.

Materials

Flowers ½ yard each of 10 fabrics

Flower centers Various fabrics to total ½ yard

Background ½ yard each of 2 fabrics

Side borders 2½ yards

Top and bottom borders 1 yard

Backing 5 yards

Binding 2 yards for lengthwise cut **OR** ⅞ yard for crosswise cut

Batting 69″ × 89″

Cutting

Flowers Cut 113 squares 6″ × 6″.

Flower centers Cut 113 squares 2″ × 2″.

Alternate squares Cut 112 squares 3″ × 3″.

Borders Measure and cut borders during construction (refer to Step 5).

Binding Cut strips 3¼″ wide lengthwise or crosswise to total 312″ after piecing the strips end to end (refer to pages 72–74).

Folding

Follow the Folding Instructions (pages 8–10) to fold the 6″ squares into 113 flowers. Each folded square should measure 3″ × 3″. Insert the 2″ squares into the centers of the folded flowers. You do not need to tack down the center squares, because their corners will be caught in the seams that you will sew later.

Construction

1. Arrange the folded flower blocks and 3″ squares as shown in the quilt photo.

2. Sew together the folded flowers and squares into 25 rows of 9 blocks.

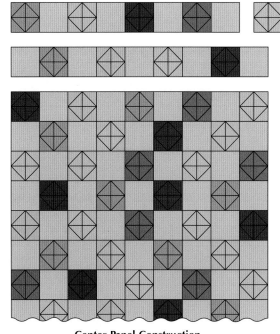

Center Panel Construction

3. Press the seam allowance of each row in alternate directions to make matching the seams easier. Sew the rows together.

4. Open the petals. Turn under the tips of the petals and stitch them in place (see Step 11, page 10). After you attach the borders and side panels, stitch the petals that overlap the borders and side panels.

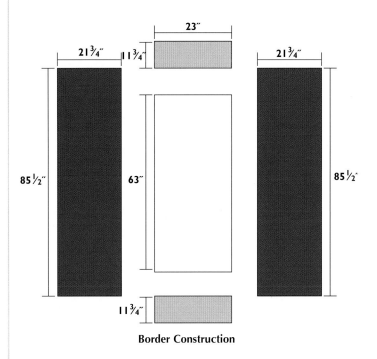

Border Construction

5. Measure the center panel before you cut the borders and adjust the size of the borders if necessary. Cut the top and bottom borders 11$\frac{3}{4}$˝ x 23˝. Cut the side border fabric in half vertically to make 2 pieces 21$\frac{3}{4}$˝ x 85$\frac{1}{2}$˝. (If your fabric is less than 43$\frac{1}{2}$˝ wide, your side borders will be slightly narrower.)

6. Attach the top and bottom borders, then the side borders (refer to pages 70–71).

7. Refer to pages 69–74 for quilting and finishing.

INSIDE-OUT FLOWER PILLOW

Inside-out Flower Pillow, 23¹/₂″ × 15¹/₂″, block size 2¹/₂″ × 2¹/₂″, Rebecca Wat

MATERIALS

Flowers Various fabrics to total ¹/₂ yard

Flower centers Various scraps

Background ¹/₄ yard

Inner border ¹/₈ yard

Outer borders ³/₈ yard

Pillow back ¹/₂ yard

Beaded ribbon 1 yard

Polyester fiberfill

CUTTING

Flowers Cut 13 squares 6″ × 6″.

Flower centers Cut 13 squares 2″ × 2″.

Background Cut 12 squares 3″ × 3″.

Inner border Cut 2 strips 2″ × 16″.

Side outer border Cut 2 strips 4¹/₂″ × 16″.

Top and bottom outer border Cut 2 strips 2″ × 13″.

Pillow back Cut 2 squares 16″ × 16″.

FOLDING

Follow the Folding Instructions (pages 8–10) to fold the 6″ squares into 13 flowers. Each folded square should measure 3″ × 3″. Insert the 2″ squares into the centers of the folded flowers. You do not need to tack down the center squares, because their corners will be caught in the seams that you will sew later.

CONSTRUCTION

1. Arrange and piece the folded flower blocks and 3″ squares to form the background as shown in the photo.

2. Attach the top and bottom outer borders to the top and bottom of the pillow. Attach the inner border and the side outer borders to the short sides of the pillow.

3. Open the petals. Turn under the tips of the petals and stitch them in place (see Step 11, page 10).

4. Refer to the photo and attach the beaded ribbon strip in place.

5. Measure the length of the pillow top and overlap the pillow back squares to achieve the same length. On one edge of each 16″ square, fold over ¹/₄″ twice and sew a narrow hem. Stitch around the edges of the pillow.

6. With right sides together, pin together the pillow top and back. Stitch. Trim the excess fabric.

7. Turn the pillow right side out. Iron-press.

8. Stuff the pillow with the fiberfill.

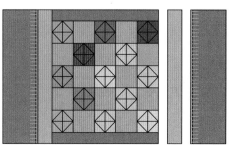

Pillow Construction

When I think about pinwheels, happy images come to mind: children, laughter, agility, vibrant colors, nice weather, good luck, and so on. A pinwheel is a simple toy that brings a smile to a young child's face and fond memories to the young at heart. Many of us have, at some time, been fascinated and amused by these colorful toys. Perhaps that's why we, as quilters, often use pinwheels as a theme for our quilts.

To add to the existing list of pinwheel designs for quilts, I have created this three-dimensional, fabric-folded pinwheel that really pops from the background. In this design, there is also a square or diamond opening (depending on the orientation of the pinwheel). You can leave this opening as is or insert some items of interest. Any way you choose, use this pinwheel design to make a special quilt—one that will bring you a simple joy, just like your very first pinwheel.

FOLDING INSTRUCTIONS

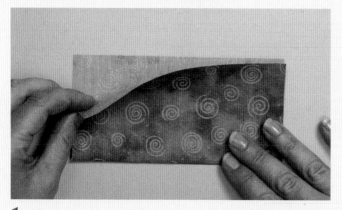

1. Place the fabric wrong side up and fold the square in half. Finger-press. Repeat in the opposite direction to form an intersection of creases.

2. With the fabric wrong side up, bring up a corner to align with the intersection. Finger-press.

3. Repeat Step 2 on the remaining 3 sides.

4. Turn over the fabric. Bring up the bottom edge to align with the intersection. Finger-press and unfold.

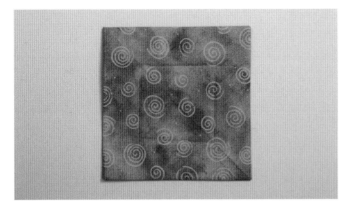

5. Repeat Step 4 on the remaining 3 sides to form a square in the center.

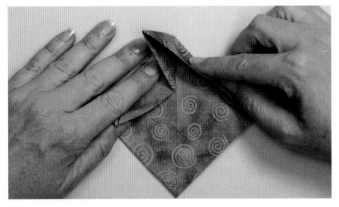

6. Use the creases of the square as a reference to bring 2 adjacent edges to the center, creating an ear between them. Press the ear to one side.

7. Turn the fabric one-quarter turn to the left and repeat Step 6.

8. Repeat Step 7 on the remaining 2 sides. To use this as an appliqué, skip to Step 18.

9. Without turning over the fabric, gently bring the 4 side triangles from the back to the front.

BLOCK CONSTRUCTION

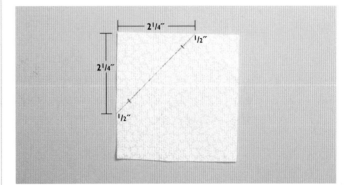

10. On the background fabric, mark a dot 2¹⁄₄˝ from one corner in each direction. Draw a line between the 2 dots to mark your sewing line. Mark another dot ¹⁄₂˝ from each end of the drawn line to mark where you will start and stop sewing.

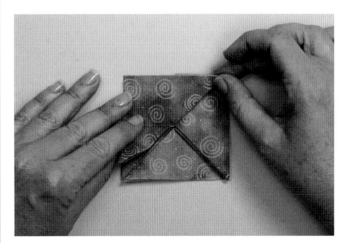

11. Before sewing the background square to a corner of the model, flip the ear out of the way.

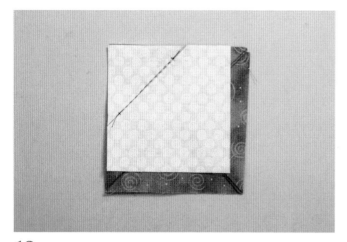

12. With right sides together, sew a background square to a corner, starting and ending about $1/2''$ from the edge and sewing through the diamond shape on the back.

13. Before you sew a background square to another corner of the model, flip the ear out of the way.

14. With right sides together, sew another background square to a corner, starting and ending about $1/2''$ from the edge.

15. Sew 2 background squares to the remaining corners.

16. Move the ear out of the way and stitch the squares together with a $1/4''$ seam, ending about $1/2''$ from the Y-shape intersection. (Don't worry about the hole in the intersection.)

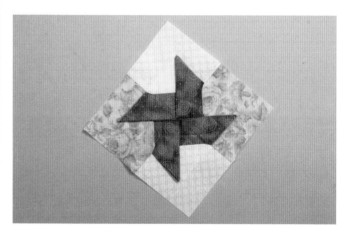

17. Arrange the pinwheel. Iron-press to set. This is one variation ready to be pieced as a block.

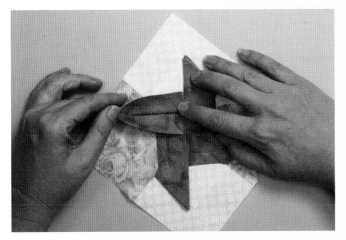

18. Open an ear. Finger-press.

19. Rotate the pinwheel one-quarter turn to the right and repeat Step 18.

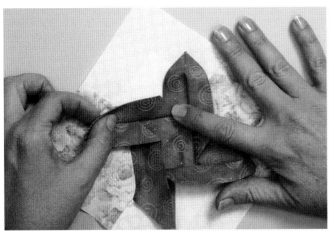

20. Rotate the model one-quarter turn to the right and repeat Step 18.

21. Rotate the model one-quarter turn to the right and repeat Step 18. Iron-press to set.

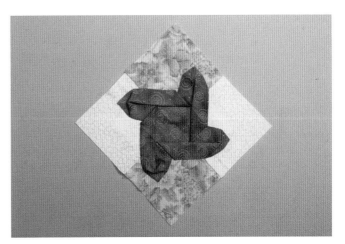

22. Stitch around the outside of the pinwheel and roll under a little bit of fabric at the tips.

Optional: Insert a contrasting fabric square and items of your choice in the center; stitch to secure.

Dancing Pinwheels I, 54$^{1}/_{2}$″ × 54$^{1}/_{2}$″, **block size: 6″ × 6″, Rebecca Wat, quilted by Denise Fabel**

When I was designing *Dancing Pinwheels I*, my first quilt using these three-dimensional pinwheels, I had to make a decision. Should I insert something into the little diamond-shaped frames at the centers of these pinwheels? Should I add some pieces of contrasting fabric, transferred fabric photos, dry flowers wrapped in translucent materials, cards with little poems or words of wisdom? Guess what I finally decided to do.

Materials

Pinwheels 5 or more fabrics to total 2¹/₂ yards

Background 1 yard each of 2 fabrics

Inner border ¹/₃ yard

Outer border and binding 2 yards

Backing 3³/₈ yards

Batting 59″ × 59″

Cutting

Pinwheels Cut 49 squares 8″ × 8″.

Background Cut 98 squares 3¹/₂″ × 3¹/₂″ from each background fabric (196 total).

Inner border Cut 6 strips 1¹/₄″ x the width of the fabric.

Outer border and binding

Cut 4 strips 6″ wide lengthwise for the border.

Cut strips 3¹/₄″ wide lengthwise for the binding to total 230″ after piecing the strips end to end (refer to pages 72–74).

Folding

Follow the Folding Instructions Steps 1–9 (pages 20–21) to fold the 8″ squares into 49 pinwheels. Each folded square should measure 4″ × 4″.

Construction

1. Follow Block Construction Steps 10–22 (pages 21–23) and sew a 3¹/₂″ square to each corner of the pinwheel.

2. Arrange and sew the blocks in rows as shown in the quilt photo.

3. Press the seam allowances of each row in alternate directions to make matching the seams easier. Sew the rows together. Press.

4. Attach the inner and outer borders (refer to pages 70–71).

5. Refer to pages 69–74 for quilting and finishing.

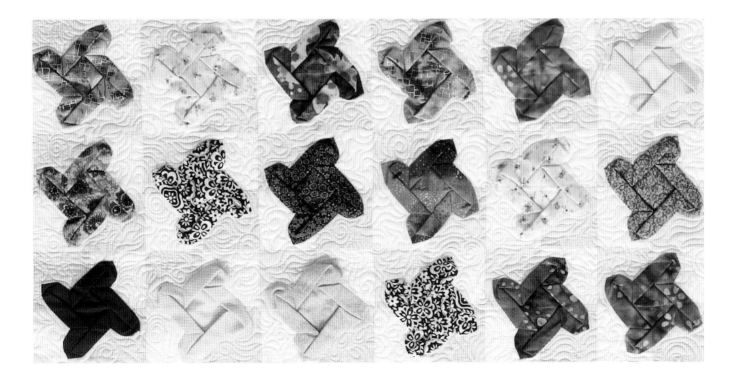

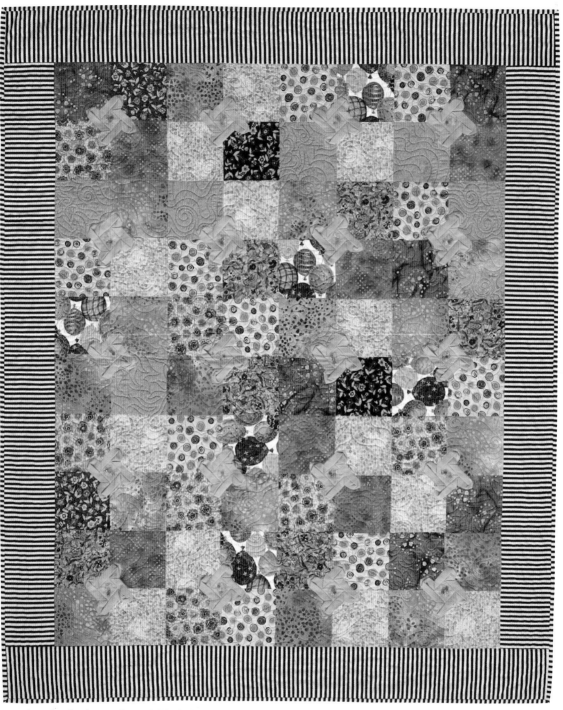

Dancing Pinwheels II, 59˝ × 71˝, block size: 12˝ × 12˝, Rebecca Wat, quilted by Denise Fabel

How I wish I could make these fabric pinwheels work like the real thing so they could really dance in the wind! Until someone comes up with a brilliant construction method, I guess I'll have to settle for some visual effects or illusions. It's okay if you don't get the visual pinwheel effects—different people see things differently. My two-year-old, for instance, keeps calling this quilt "zebra" because of the striped borders!

Materials

Pinwheels $1\frac{1}{8}$ yards

Pinwheel centers $\frac{1}{4}$ yard

Background 5 or more fabrics to total 3 yards

Border and binding 2 yards

Backing $4\frac{1}{4}$ yards

Batting $63'' \times 75''$

Beads 100–120 (approximately 6–7mm in size)

Cutting

Pinwheels Cut 20 squares $8'' \times 8''$.

Pinwheel centers Cut 20 squares $2\frac{1}{2}'' \times 2\frac{1}{2}''$.

Background Cut 80 squares $6\frac{1}{2}'' \times 6\frac{1}{2}''$.

Border Cut strips 6″ wide lengthwise or crosswise, depending on the fabric pattern.

Binding Cut strips $3\frac{1}{4}''$ wide lengthwise or crosswise, depending on the fabric pattern, to total 272″ after piecing strips end to end (refer to pages 72–74).

Folding

Follow the Folding Instructions Steps 1–9 (pages 20–21) to fold the 8″ squares into 20 pinwheels. Each folded square should measure $4'' \times 4''$.

Construction

1. For each block, follow the Block Construction Steps 10–22 (pages 21–23) and sew a $6\frac{1}{2}''$ square to each corner of the pinwheels. Insert the center squares and add the beads.

2. Arrange and sew the blocks in rows as shown in the quilt photo.

3. Press the seam allowances of each row in alternate directions to make matching the seams easier. Sew the rows together. Press.

4. Attach the borders (refer to pages 70–71).

5. Refer to pages 69–74 for quilting and finishing.

Pinwheel Pillow, 18″ × 18″, Rebecca Wat

MATERIALS

Pinwheels Various fabrics to total ¹/₂ yard

Background ¹/₃ yard each of 2 fabrics

Sheer or net fabric ¹/₄ yard

Beads 20 to 30 (approximately 6–8mm in size)

Beaded fringe 2¹/₄ yards

Pillow backing ¹/₂ yard

Polyester fiberfill or **18″ pillow form**

Pretreated fabric sheets for inkjet printers

CUTTING

Pinwheels Cut 9 squares 7¹/₂″ × 7¹/₂″.

Background Cut 18 squares 3¹/₂″ × 3¹/₂″ from each fabric (36 total).

Pillow backing Cut 2 rectangles 14″ × 18¹/₂″.

FOLDING

Follow the Folding Instructions Steps 1–9 (pages 20–21) to fold the 7¹/₂″ squares into 9 pinwheels.

CONSTRUCTION

1. Print your photos on the pretreated fabric, according to the manufacturer's instructions. The photos will need to be large enough so that you can trim them to 2″ squares set on point.

2. Cut 5 squares 2″ × 2″ from the printed fabric photos.

3. Insert and sew the 5 photos to the centers of 5 pinwheels.

4. Insert and sew the sheer or net fabric to the remaining 4 pinwheels. Before you sew the last opening closed, place beads under the fabric.

5. Arrange and piece the 3¹/₂″ squares to form the background.

6. Pin and stitch the pinwheels onto the background. (Yes, you can use these pinwheels as appliqués.)

7. With the pillow top right side up, pin the fringe along the edge of the pillow top, overlapping ¹/₂″ where the ends meet. The fringe will fall toward the inside of the pillow. When the pillow is sewn and turned, the fringe will be on the outside.

8. On the short edge of each backing rectangle, fold over ¹/₄″ twice and sew a narrow hem. Measure the length of the pillow top. Overlap the pillow back rectangles to achieve the same length.

9. With right sides together, pin the pillow top and back together. Stitch the front to the back. Trim excess fabric.

10. Turn the pillow right side out. Iron-press.

11. Stuff the pillow with fiberfill or a pillow form.

es, it looks just like the traditional Bow Tie block. But when you touch this block or look at it at an angle, you immediately notice the dimension and unique texture—one that even allows you to run your fingers underneath. This is a very different Bow Tie block, a brand-new fabric origami block. A piece of square fabric and a few stitches are all it takes. If you like, you can build on this basic block by adding contrasting fabrics or by stuffing the Bow Ties. This process is so amazing and dramatic, it will make you feel like a magician!

2. Turn over the square so the wrong side is up. These are the creases you'll pick up in Steps 3–9.

FOLDING INSTRUCTIONS

1. Place the fabric right side up and fold the square in half. Finger-press. Repeat in the opposite direction to form an intersection of creases.

3. Pick up the left half of the horizontal crease and align it with the top left corner.

4. Pin the crease to the top left corner.

5. Rotate the fabric one-quarter turn to the right. Pick up the left half of the horizontal crease and align it with the top left corner.

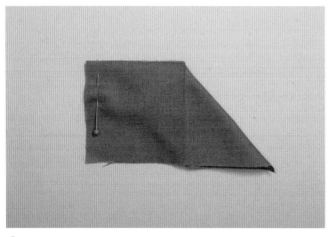

6. Pin the crease to the top left corner.

7. Rotate the fabric one-quarter turn to the right. Pick up the left half of the horizontal crease and align it with the top left corner.

8. Pin the crease to the top left corner.

9. Rotate the fabric one-quarter turn to the right. Pick up the left half of the horizontal crease and align it with the top left corner.

10. Pin the crease to the top left corner. A puff is formed at the center.

11. Press the puff to form a diamond shape. Remove the pins and iron-press.

12. Insert a threaded needle in the center of one side of the diamond to pick up a little bit of fabric.

13. Repeat Step 12 on the remaining 3 sides.

14. Return to where you first started sewing.

15. Pull the thread to gather all the sides to the center. Make a knot and cut the thread.

16. Spread out the fabric to its full extent to form a square.

19. For variation, place a piece of lace or contrasting fabric under the bow.

17. Arrange the pleats as shown.

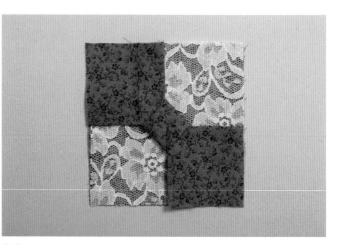

20. Repeat Step 19 on the other side.

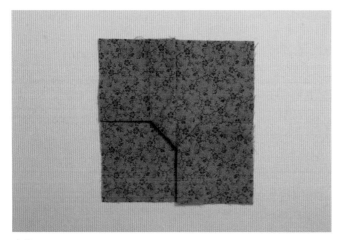

18. Turn over the fabric and iron-press. You can now piece this as a regular quilt block.

21. Fold the block in half.

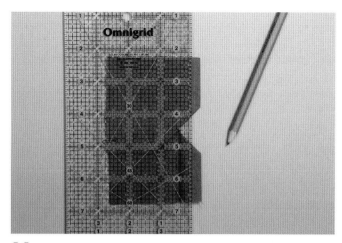

22. Sew with a ¼″ seam allowance, catching the lace or contrasting fabric in the seam.

23. Cut off the excess thread. Repeat Step 22 on the other side to secure the lace or fabric under the Bow Tie.

24. You can now piece this as a regular quilt block.

A PIECE OF THE SKY

A Piece of the Sky, 68″ × 87^1/$_2$″, **block size: 3^1/$_4$″ × 3^1/$_4$″, Rebecca Wat, quilted by Denise Fabel**

Photo by Sharon Risedorph

nce in a while, I want to make a different kind of quilt—one that does not require any thought about color combinations or that does not generate anxiety about not finding all the fabrics I need. I just pick a color of fabric that I want to work with, sit down with a cup of tea, and start exercising my fingers.

MATERIALS

Blocks and binding 11 yards

Backing $5^1/4$ yards

Batting $72'' \times 91''$

CUTTING

Blocks Cut 520 squares $5'' \times 5''$.

Binding Cut approximately 120 squares $3^1/2'' \times 3^1/2''$ for prairie points.

FOLDING

Hint: To save time, do each of the following steps by batch.

1. Follow the Folding Instructions Steps 1–11 (pages 29–31) to fold the 5″ squares into 520 folded squares.

2. Follow the Folding Instructions Steps 12–15 (page 31) to stitch the folded squares.

3. Open the folded squares and press, according to the Folding Instructions Steps 16–18 (page 32). Each folded square should measure $3^3/4'' \times 3^3/4''$.

CONSTRUCTION

1. Sew 20 squares together to form each row. Make 26 rows.

2. Press the seam allowances of each row in alternate directions to make matching the seams easier.

3. Sew the rows together. Press.

4. Make the prairie points.

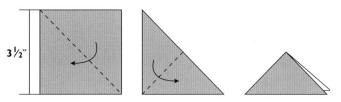

Fold $3^1/2''$ square. Iron-press.

5. Line up the folded triangles evenly along the edge of the quilt top and pin or baste them in place. Stitch around the edge of the quilt $1/4''$ from the outside edge.

Arrange triangles along outside edge.

6. Refer to page 72 to layer and baste the quilt.

7. Quilt by hand or machine leaving at least $1/4''$ from the edge unquilted to leave room for finishing. Trim the batting to align with the edge of the quilt top. Take care not to cut the backing.

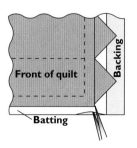

Trim batting.

8. Trim the backing about ½˝ larger than the batting.

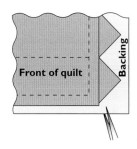

Trim backing.

9. Wrap the backing around the batting and pin.

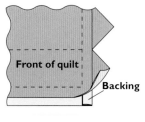

Wrap backing.

10. Hand stitch the backing to the prairie points on the back side of the quilt top.

Stitch.

Black Tie, 38¹/₄˝ × 38¹/₄˝, **block size: 4¹/₂˝ × 4¹/₂˝, Rebecca Wat**

hink of these three-dimensional Bow Tie blocks as construction blocks you can add to. In this case, I chose white lace because it provides an interesting contrast—both in texture and in color—to the black-tone Bow Ties. If black and white are not the colors you want to combine, just replace them with two other colors or two shades of the same color. You can also easily adapt this pattern to a different size to come up with that bedcover, coffee-table quilt, throw for the sofa, or table runner that you always wanted.

MATERIALS

Bow Ties 5 or more fabrics to total 2 yards

Lace 1⅛ yards

Border and center block ½ yard

Backing 1¼ yards

Binding 1¼ yards for lengthwise cut **OR** ½ yard for crosswise cut

Batting 42″ × 42″

CUTTING

Bow Ties Cut 60 squares 6½″ × 6½″.

Lace Cut 120 squares 3¼″ × 3¼″.

Border Cut 5 squares 7⅝″ × 7⅝″. Cut each square diagonally twice for the side triangles. Cut 2 squares 4⅛″ × 4⅛″. Cut each square diagonally once for the corner triangles.

Center block Cut 1 square 5″ × 5″.

Binding Cut strips 3¼″ wide lengthwise or crosswise to total 166″ after piecing the strips end to end (refer to pages 72–74).

FOLDING

Hint: To save time, do each of the following steps by batch.

1. Follow the Folding Instructions Steps 1–11 (pages 29–31) to fold the 6½″ squares into 60 folded squares.

2. Follow the Folding Instructions Steps 12–15 (page 31) to stitch the folded squares.

3. Open the folded squares and press, according to the Folding Instructions Steps 16–18 (page 32). Each folded square should measure 5″ × 5″.

4. Tuck a pair of 3¼″ squares under each folded bow, as explained in the Folding Instructions Steps 19–20 (page 32).

5. Sew the 3¼″ squares in place, as explained in the Folding Instructions Steps 21–24 (pages 32–33).

CONSTRUCTION

1. Arrange all the pieces as shown in the quilt photo.

2. Sew the pieces together in diagonal rows.

3. Press the seam allowances of each row in alternate directions to make matching the seams easier.

4. Sew the rows together. Press.

5. Use a quilting ruler and a rotary cutter to square the quilt. Trim the side triangles.

6. Refer to pages 69–74 for quilting and finishing.

Quilt Construction

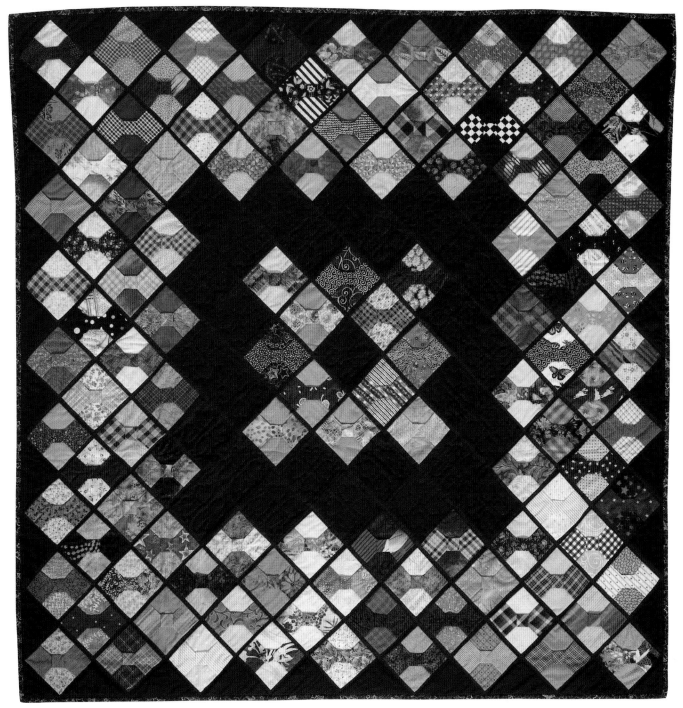

Bow Tie Medley, 71″ × 71″, **block size: 4^1/$_2$″ × 4^1/$_2$″, Rebecca Wat**

onceptually, *Bow Tie Medley* is the exact opposite of *A Piece of the Sky.* With more than 100 fabrics in this quilt, each Bow Tie block is different. The good news is that you will always have a foolproof color combination. As Freddy Moran, author of *Freddy's House,* put it: "Ten colors don't work, but a hundred do!" What you have to make sure of is that you have enough different fabrics. By the way, it is fun to match up Bow Ties with background fabrics—a process similar to finding the right shirt for a tie and vice versa.

MATERIALS

Bow Ties 20 or more fabrics to total 4 yards

Contrasting fabrics 20 or more fabrics to total 2 yards

Background 3 yards

Backing $4^{1}/_{4}$ yards

Binding 2 yards for lengthwise cut **OR** $^{7}/_{8}$ yard for crosswise cut

Batting $75'' \times 75''$

CUTTING

Bow Ties Cut 116 squares $6^{1}/_{2}'' \times 6^{1}/_{2}''$.

Contrasting fabrics Cut 232 squares $3^{1}/_{4}'' \times 3^{1}/_{4}''$. (Cut pairs of squares from the same fabric for each block.)

Background and sashing

Cut 29 squares $5'' \times 5''$.

Cut 162 rectangles $1'' \times 5''$.

Cut 22 strips $1''$ x the width of the fabric.

Cut 8 squares $9^{1}/_{8}'' \times 9^{1}/_{8}''$. Cut each square diagonally twice for side triangles.

Cut 2 squares $4^{7}/_{8}'' \times 4^{7}/_{8}''$. Cut each square diagonally once for corner triangles.

Binding Cut strips $3^{1}/_{4}''$ wide lengthwise or crosswise to total $296''$ after piecing the strips end to end (refer to pages 72–74).

FOLDING

Hint: To save time, do each of the following steps by batch.

1. Follow the Folding Instructions Steps 1–11 (pages 29–31) to fold the $6^{1}/_{2}''$ squares into 116 folded squares.

2. Follow the Folding Instructions Steps 12–15 (page 31) to stitch the folded squares.

3. Open the folded squares and press, according to the Folding Instructions Steps 16–18 (page 32). Each folded square should measure $5'' \times 5''$.

4. Tuck a pair of $3^{1}/_{4}''$ squares under each folded bow, as shown in the Folding Instructions Steps 19–20 (page 32).

5. Sew the $3^{1}/_{4}''$ squares in place, as shown in the Folding Instructions Steps 21–24 (pages 32–33).

CONSTRUCTION

1. Arrange all the pieces as shown in the quilt photo.

2. Sew together by row the Bow Tie blocks, background blocks, short sashing pieces, and side triangles. Press toward the sashing.

3. Piece the $1''$-wide sashing strips together end to end as necessary.

4. Sew the rows together.

5. Use a quilting ruler and rotary cutter to square the quilt. Trim the side triangles.

6. Refer to pages 69–74 for quilting and finishing.

Quilt Construction

Three-Dimensional Petals

There are two fabric-folding techniques in this chapter: Fortune Cookie Petals and Diamond Petals. Fortune Cookie Petals are similar to the petals of the Inside-out Flowers, both in appearance and in structure. However, Fortune Cookie Petals are appliqués made individually, whereas Inside-out Flowers are blocks made for piecing. By making the Fortune Cookie Petals individually, you can customize the shape and size of each petal (or leaf) to achieve any special image of a flower you have in mind. The Fortune Cookie Petals technique makes this process easy, and the end result is three-dimensional.

Diamond Petals are polygon flowers (a ready-to-go appliqué by itself) without the base. Make Diamond Petals by starting with a pentagon. Then cut out the base of the flower. The result is a flower appliqué with remarkably even, clean-cut petals. [*Note:* If you have *Fantastic Fabric Folding* (see Resources, page 79), you can use this technique with any of the polygon flower shapes in that book.]

FOLDING INSTRUCTIONS
FORTUNE COOKIE PETALS

1. Place a rectangle right side up.

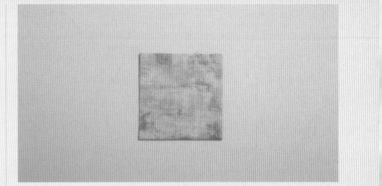

2. Fold the rectangle in half. Finger-press.

3. Fold down a corner to form a triangle. Finger-press.

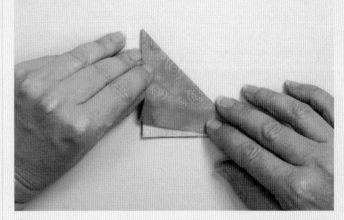

4. Turn over the fabric and repeat Step 3 on the other side, aligning the triangles.

5. The resulting triangle has an open end.

6. Draw a line from the open end to the adjacent side. This is the sewing line.

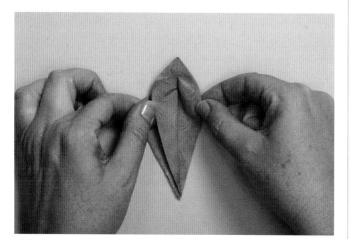

7. You can customize the shape of the petal by adjusting the angle of the sewing line. Open the petal to check if it's the shape you want.

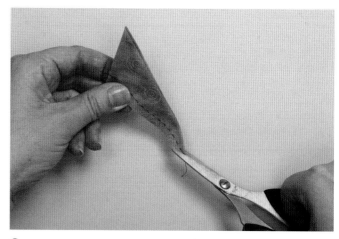

8. Stitch along the sewing line. To save time, sew by the batch, like chain piecing. Trim off the excess fabric.

9. Open the petal. Use it like any appliqué.

Optional: Try stuffing oversized petals with batting to dramatize the three-dimensional effect. After you partially sew down the petals, stuff them with batting or bits of polyester fiberfill.

FOLDING INSTRUCTIONS
DIAMOND PETALS

1. Use the template provided on page 75 or 76 to cut a pentagon. With the fabric wrong side up, fold it in half 3 times to form an intersection of creases.

2. Bring up the bottom edge to align with the intersection in the center of the pentagon. Fold and finger-press. Open the fabric.

3. Repeat Step 2 on the remaining 4 sides to form a pentagon in the center.

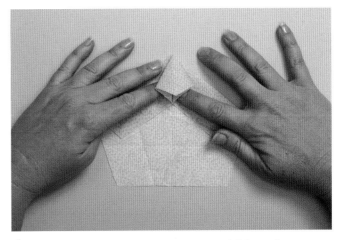

4. Use the creases as a reference to fold 2 adjacent sides inward, creating an ear between them.

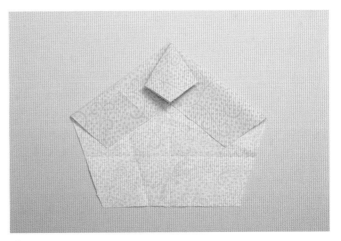

5. Finger-press the ear to form a kite shape.

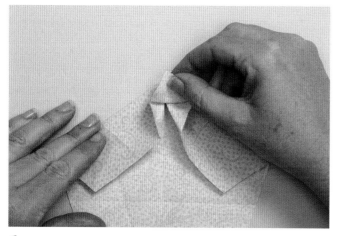

6. Open the kite shape.

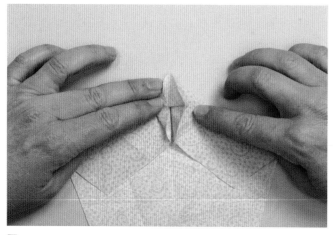

7. Fold all the raw edges to the center to form a diamond shape.

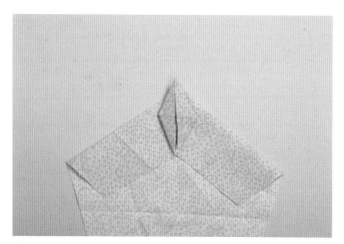

8. Finger-press.

9. Flip the tip of the diamond-shaped petal to the center. Pin or stitch to secure the tip to the center.

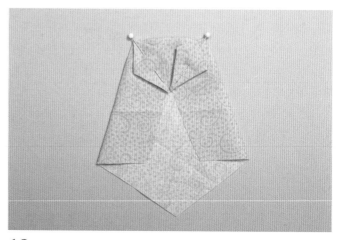

10. Repeat to form diamond petals on the remaining 4 sides.

11. Iron-press to set the shape. Stitch the center. Cover the center with a button or an appliqué so that you can use your Diamond Petal like a regular appliqué.

12. For variation, cut out the base connecting the petals.

Back view

Front view

LAZY DAISIES

Lazy Daisies, 36″ × 55″, Rebecca Wat, quilted by Denise Fabel

The combination of oriental theme fabrics and denim-look cotton—an integration of elements of the east and the west—makes this quilt special. I would describe it as eclectic. When you don't have the luxury of time but still want to satisfy your creative needs, perhaps this quilt is the answer, as it is one of those quick weekend projects you can enjoy and be proud of.

Materials

Flower petals $\frac{1}{2}$ yard

Flower centers $\frac{1}{8}$ yard

Flower stems $4\frac{1}{2}$ yards of ribbon or trim

Background

    Light fabric $\frac{7}{8}$ yard

    Dark fabric 2 yards

Backing $1\frac{3}{4}$ yards

Binding 1 yard for lengthwise cut **OR** $\frac{5}{8}$ yard for cross-wise cut

Batting $40˝ \times 59˝$

Cutting

Flower petals Cut 17 rectangles $4˝ \times 8˝$.

Flower centers Use Template A (page 74) to cut 3 ovals.

Background

    Light fabric Cut 10 strips $2\frac{1}{2}˝$ wide × the width of the fabric.

    Dark fabric Cut 10 strips $2\frac{1}{2}˝$ wide × the width of the fabric.

    Measure and cut the top and bottom backgrounds during construction (refer to Steps 4–6).

Binding Cut strips $3\frac{1}{4}˝$ wide crosswise or lengthwise to total 194˝ after piecing the strips end to end (refer to pages 72–74).

Folding

Follow the Fortune Cookie Petals Folding Instructions (pages 41–42) to fold the $4˝ \times 8˝$ rectangles into 17 petals.

Construction

Background

1. Sew the dark and light strips together as shown, alternating dark and light fabrics. Press the seams toward the dark fabric. Make 2 strip sets.

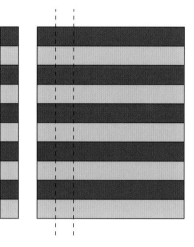

Background Construction

2. Cut 18 segments $2\frac{1}{2}˝$ wide from the sewn strips.

3. Place the strips in alternate directions to achieve a checkerboard pattern. Pin the strips together, nesting the seams. Stitch and press.

4. Measure the exact width of the checkerboard background (it should be approximately $36\frac{1}{2}˝$).

5. Cut the background fabric to the width from Step 4 × $10\frac{1}{2}˝$. Sew to the top of the checkerboard background.

6. Cut the background fabric to the width from Step 4 × $25\frac{1}{2}˝$. Sew to the bottom of the checkerboard background.

Flowers

1. Arrange the petals, the ovals, and the ribbon or trim as shown in the quilt photo.

2. Pin and baste them to the background.

3. Appliqué everything in place.

4. Refer to pages 69–74 for quilting and finishing.

BLUE SAPPHIRE II

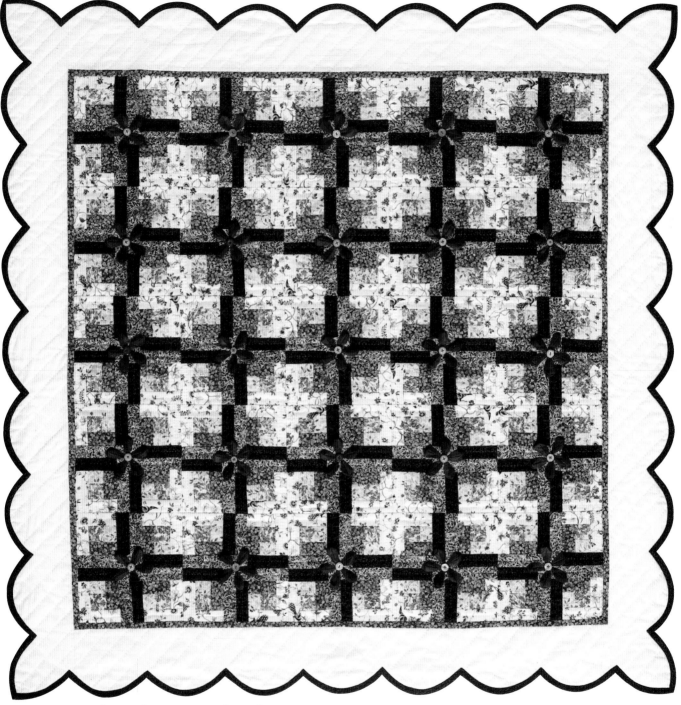

Blue Sapphire II, 54^1/$_2$˝ × 54^1/$_2$˝, **block size: 8^1/$_2$˝ × 8^1/$_2$˝, Rebecca Wat**

ike its predecessor *Blue Sapphire I* (page 13), *Blue Sapphire II* is a Log Cabin quilt. In this one, a flower appliqué is stitched on top of each Log Cabin block, giving it a softer look. The scalloped binding echoes the curves of the flowers. The result is a crisp, gemlike quilt.

MATERIALS

Fabric suggestions for Log Cabin blocks: 3 lighter-color fabrics and 4 darker-color fabrics

Flowers ¾ yard

Log Cabin blocks

Light fabrics
½ yard each of 3 fabrics

Dark fabrics
⅓ yard of fabric 1
½ yard of fabric 2
½ yard of fabric 5
⅝ yard of fabric 6

Inner border ½ yard for crosswise cut

Outer border 1⅝ yards for lengthwise cut **OR** 1¼ yards for crosswise cut

Backing 3½ yards

Binding ⅔ yard

Batting 59″ × 59″

Buttons 25

CUTTING

Flowers Cut 10 strips 1½″ wide x the width of the fabric and cut into 125 rectangles 1½″ × 3″.

Log Cabin centers Cut 5 light strips 1¾″ wide x the width of the fabric and cut into 100 squares 1¾″ × 1¾″.

Log Cabin logs Cut all strips 1½″ crosswise. You will need:

4 strips of fabric 1 (dark)
6 strips of fabric 2 (dark)
8 strips of fabric 3 (light)
10 strips of fabric 4 (light)
8 strips of fabric 5 (dark)
10 strips of fabric 6 (dark)

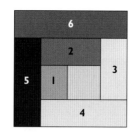

Inner border Cut 6 strips 1″ wide x the width of the fabric.

Outer border Cut 4 strips 6″ wide lengthwise **OR** 6 strips 6″ wide crosswise.

Binding Cut bias strips 2″ wide to total 250″ (refer to page 73 for continuous bias).

FOLDING

Follow the Diamond Petal Folding Instructions Steps 1–12 (pages 43–45) to fold the 1½″ × 3″ rectangles into 125 petals.

CONSTRUCTION

1. For each Log Cabin block, sew 1½″-wide strips to one side of the center block and continue to add strips as shown. (Also refer to Quick Cutting and Assembly Method on page 15.)

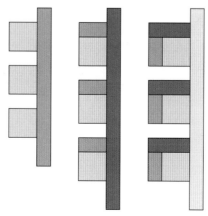

Log Cabin Block Assembly

2. Sew 4 blocks together as shown.

Block Construction

3. Arrange and baste the petals in place. Appliqué them in place.

4. Attach the buttons to the centers of the flowers.

5. Sew the block sections together by row. Press the seams in opposite directions. Sew the rows together. Press.

6. Attach the inner and outer borders (refer to pages 70–71).

7. Use the templates from page 76 to mark the scalloped border. Do not cut until you have completed the quilting.

8. Refer to pages 69–74 for quilting and finishing.

9. Refer to page 73 for scalloped binding.

DAFFODILS

Daffodils, $39^1/2″ \times 52^1/2″$, **Rebecca Wat, quilted by Denise Fabel**

What I love about this quilt is its contrast in color—a very bright white is used against a flat brownish-green background. The size of the daffodils is exaggerated to further enhance this effect, as well as to highlight the quilt's theme. Just like when you are doing a real flower arrangement, deciding where to place the daffodils is a fun process. For variations, try combining different kinds of flowers in various sizes.

MATERIALS

Flowers ⅝ yard

Background

    Center ⅓ yard

    Sashing ¼ yard

    Top and bottom 1⅛ yards

Borders and binding 1½ yards

Batting 43″ × 56″

Buttons 8

CUTTING

Flowers Use Template F (page 76) to cut 8 pentagons.

Background

    Center Cut 1 rectangle 9″ × 28″.

    Sashing Cut 2 rectangles 3″ × 28″.

    Top Cut 1 rectangle 9½″ × 28″.

    Bottom Cut 1 rectangle 18½″ × 28″.

Borders Cut 4 strips 6″ wide lengthwise.

Binding Cut strips 3¼″ wide lengthwise to total 196″ after piecing the strips end to end (refer to pages 72–74).

FOLDING

Follow the Diamond Petal Folding Instructions Steps 1–12 (pages 43–45) to fold the pentagons into 8 flowers.

CONSTRUCTION

1. Arrange and sew all the background pieces together.

Background Construction

2. Arrange the flowers as shown in the quilt photo.

3. Pin and baste the flowers to the background.

4. Appliqué everything in place.

5. Sew on buttons or create flower centers, as desired.

6. Attach the borders (refer to pages 70–71).

7. Refer to pages 69–74 for quilting and finishing.

TO MILLENNIUM

To Millennium, 64^1/$_2$″ × 64^1/$_2$″, **block size: 21^1/$_2$″ × 21^1/$_2$″, Rebecca Wat, quilted by Virginia Dunlap**

I made this quilt to commemorate the arrival of the year 2000. Unlike my other quilts, I used several different fabric flowers in this one quilt: *Inside-out Flowers, Diamond Petal,* and *Fortune Cookie Petals.* It may be a little more time-consuming for beginning fabric folders to learn three different folding techniques for one quilt, but by using the different flowers, you get a result that is much more interesting than using just one folding technique.

Materials

Background 5 yards

Inside-out Flowers Various fabrics to total ½ yard

Pentagon Flowers ⅓ yard each of 6 fabrics

Large Daisies 1 yard each of 2 fabrics

Small Daisies ¼ yard each of 2 or more fabrics

Daisy centers Scraps of various fabrics or 49 buttons ½″ in diameter and 25 buttons ¼″ in diameter

Leaves and flourishes 1 yard each of 2 fabrics

Backing 4 yards

Binding 2 yards for lengthwise cut **OR** ⅞ yard for crosswise cut

Batting 68″ × 68″

Cutting

Background

Cut 8 squares 24″ × 24″.

Cut 2 squares 14½″ × 14½″, then cut diagonally twice.

Inside-out Flowers (center block)

Flowers Cut 13 squares 6″ × 6″.

Background Cut 12 squares 3″ × 3″.

Daisies (corner blocks)

Cut 294 rectangles 2″ × 4″.

Cut 125 rectangles 1″ × 2″.

Pentagon flowers (in-between blocks) Use Template G (page 75) to cut 60 flowers.

Leaves and flourishes Use the template patterns on pages 74–75 to cut 16 B, 16 C, 4 D, 8 E, and 8 F.

Binding Cut strips 3¼″ wide lengthwise or crosswise to total 272″ after piecing the strips end to end (refer to pages 72–74).

Folding

1. *Inside-out Flowers:* Follow the Folding Instructions Steps 1–8 (pages 8–9) to fold the 6″ squares into 13 Inside-out Flowers.

2. *Daisies:* Follow the Fortune Cookie Petal Folding Instructions Steps 1–9 (pages 41–42) to fold the 2″ × 4″ rectangles into large petals to make 49 large flowers and the 1″ × 2″ rectangles into small petals to make 25 small flowers.

3. *Pentagon flowers:* Follow the Diamond Petal Folding Instructions Steps 1–11 (pages 43–45) to fold the pentagons into 60 flowers.

Construction

Refer to page 10 *for appliqué instructions.*

1. For the center block:

Arrange and sew the pieces together.

Press the seams toward the triangles.

Follow the Inside-out Flower Folding Instruction Steps 10–11 (page 10) to fold and stitch the petals in place.

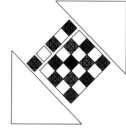

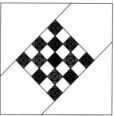

Center Block Construction

2. For the corner blocks:

Pin and baste the petals in place. Appliqué in place.

Appliqué the little circles to the centers of the flowers.

Pin and baste the flourishes. Appliqué in place.

3. For the in-between blocks:

Pin and baste the pentagon flowers in place. Appliqué in place.

Appliqué little circles or sew buttons to the centers of the flowers.

Pin and baste decorative brush-stroke designs. Appliqué in place.

4. Square up all blocks to 22″x 22″. Arrange and piece the 9 blocks together into rows.

5. Press the seam allowances of each row in alternate directions to make matching the seams easier. Sew the rows together. Press.

6. Refer to pages 69–74 for quilting and finishing.

LAZY DAISIES PILLOW

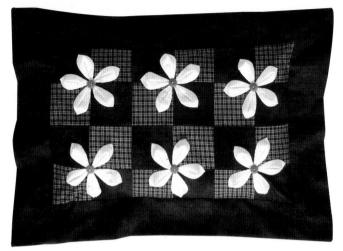

Lazy Daisies Pillow, 24″ × 18″, Rebecca Wat

MATERIALS

Fabric suggestions

Flowers ¼ yard

Background ¼ yard each of 2 fabrics

Borders and pillow back 1 yard

Buttons 6

Polyester fiberfill

CUTTING

Flowers Cut 30 rectangles 2″ × 4″.

Background Cut 24 squares (12 from each fabric) 3½″ × 3½″.

Borders

   Cut 2 strips 3½″ × 30″.

   Cut 2 strips 3½″ × 24″.

Pillow back Cut 2 rectangles 16″ × 18″.

FOLDING

Follow the Fortune Cookie Petal Folding Instructions (pages 41–42) to fold the 2″ × 4″ rectangles into 30 petals.

CONSTRUCTION

1. Arrange and piece the 3½″ squares to form the background.

2. Pin and appliqué the flower petals onto the background.

3. Attach the buttons.

4. Attach the borders and miter the corners (refer to pages 70–71).

5. On the 18″ edge of each back rectangle, fold over ¼″ twice and sew a narrow hem. Measure the length of the pillow top. Overlap the pillow back rectangles to achieve the same length. Stitch.

6. With right sides together, pin and sew the pillow top and back together. Trim excess fabric.

7. Turn the pillow right side out. Iron-press the border and corners. Stitch in-the-ditch between the background and the border to form the flange.

8. Stuff the pillow with fiberfill.

Simply Pleats

leating is the most basic and frequently used form of fabric manipulation. In this chapter, you will learn how to use the simple technique of gathering fabric and anchoring it with a few stitches to create unique and beautiful quilts.

When making pleats—from arranging them neatly in a row to randomly throwing them in all forms, shapes, and directions—there is plenty of room to stretch your imagination. If you pleat vertically and horizontally in an alternating fashion, you will see curves form between the pleats. To enhance the visual impact of the curves, simply make the pleats in blocks of different colors. Furthermore, systematic grouping of colors can yield very different, interesting results. The patterns shown here, *Butterflies Chase* and *Autumn Leaves,* are just two examples. You can use similar techniques to create many more new patterns as you continue to explore and experiment with pleats.

FOLDING INSTRUCTIONS

1. Arrange and piece the fabric squares according to the design.

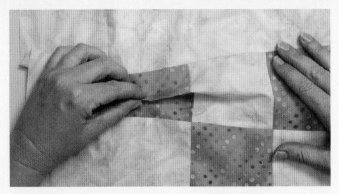

2. Start from a corner of the quilt and gather the fabric to the center to make 3 or 4 pleats. Stitch to hold the pleats together.

3. Move to an adjacent block and repeat Step 2 in the opposite direction. Repeat for the remaining blocks.

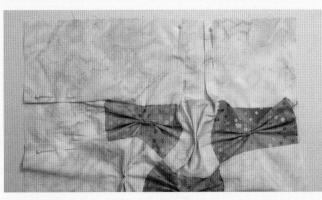

4. To straighten the border, make pleats as shown. Then pin and sew the pleats together.

AUTUMN LEAVES

Autumn Leaves, 46˝ × 54˝, **Rebecca Wat**

*I*magine one autumn morning, you are walking through a path lined with maple trees on both sides. The fallen leaves—in yellow, orange, plum, red, and brown—form a beautiful carpet under your feet. You pause to marvel at the lavish colors of nature,

look up to catch sight of some falling leaves, and then close your eyes to give thanks. It is a perfect moment of solitude and rest that you have longed for. Now you can make a quilt to capture and remind yourself of such a moment.

MATERIALS

Leaves (brighter fabrics) 8 fat quarters **OR** ¹/₄ yard each of 8 fabrics

Background (lighter fabrics) ¹/₂ yard each of 6 or more fabrics

Border and binding 2 yards

Backing 3¹/₄ yards

Batting 50˝ × 58˝

CUTTING

Leaves Cut 80 squares 5˝ × 5˝ from brighter fabrics.

Background

Cut 48 squares 5˝ × 5˝ from lighter fabrics.

Cut 4 squares 14˝ × 14˝, then cut diagonally twice into 16 side triangles (you will only need 14).

Cut 1 square 7¹/₄˝ × 7¹/₄˝, then cut diagonally twice into 4 corner triangles.

Border Cut 4 strips 6˝ wide lengthwise.

Binding Cut strips 3¹/₄˝ wide lengthwise to total 212˝ after piecing the strips end to end (refer to pages 72–74).

CONSTRUCTION

1. Sew 4 squares together into blocks. Make 20 bright leaf blocks and 12 background blocks.

2. Arrange the blocks as shown in the construction diagram and the quilt photo.

3. Sew the blocks together into rows.

4. Press the seam allowances of each row in alternate directions to make matching the seams easier. Sew the rows together. Press.

5. Follow the Folding Instructions (page 55) to create pleats for each square.

6. Straighten the borders by creating even pleats on the border triangles. Stitch the pleats in place.

7. Attach the borders (refer to pages 70–71).

8. Refer to pages 69–74 for quilting and finishing.

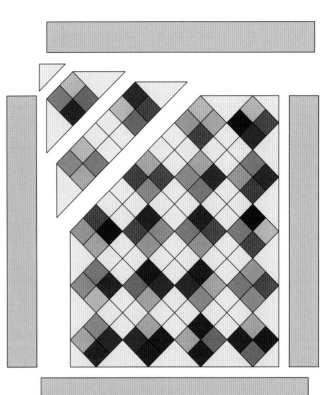

Quilt Construction

BUTTERFLIES CHASE

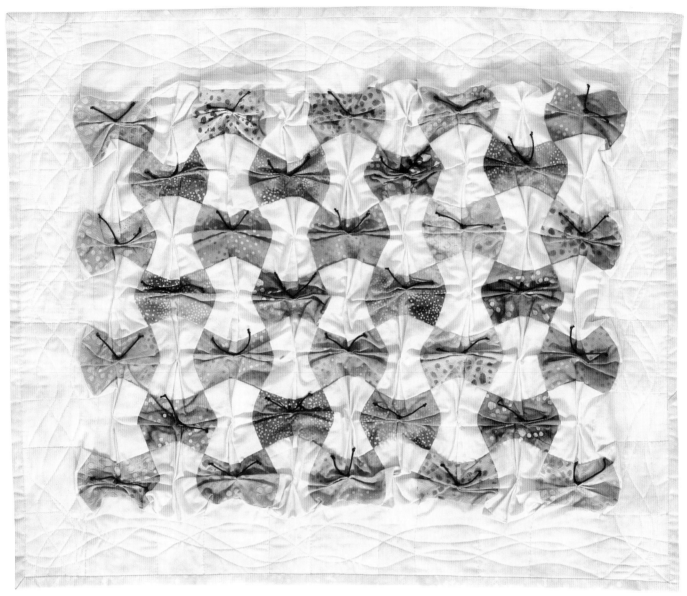

Butterflies Chase, 36″ × 32″, **Rebecca Wat**

What an easy way to make butterflies in a quilt! Simply cut the squares, piece them together, and pleat them up. It's so easy, you can make this quilt in a single day. If you like, you can adapt this pattern to make a larger quilt with perhaps 100 butterflies, all in vibrant colors. It really doesn't take much time to have these enchanting creatures bobbing up and down in your house.

Materials

Butterflies 3 fat quarters *OR* ¼ yard each of 3 fabrics

Cording for butterfly antennas 5 yards

Background ¾ yard

Borders 1¼ yards

Backing 1¼ yards

Binding ½ yard

Batting 40″ × 36″

Cutting

Butterflies

Cut 32 squares 5″ × 5″.

Cut cording into 32 segments 5″ long.

Background Cut 31 squares 5″ × 5″.

Border Cut 4 strips 5″ wide lengthwise.

Binding Cut strips 3¼″ wide crosswise to total 148″ after piecing the strips together end to end (refer to pages 72–74).

Construction

1. Arrange the blocks as shown in the quilt photo.

2. Sew the blocks together into rows.

3. Press the seam allowances of each row in alternate directions to make matching the seams easier. Sew the rows together. Press.

4. Attach the borders (refer to pages 70–71).

5. Follow the Folding Instructions (page 55) to create pleats for each square.

6. Straighten the borders by evenly creating inverted pleats. Stitch the pleats in place.

7. Make antennas for the butterflies.

Butterfly antennas
Make 2 square knots with cording. Secure cording
with a few stitches.

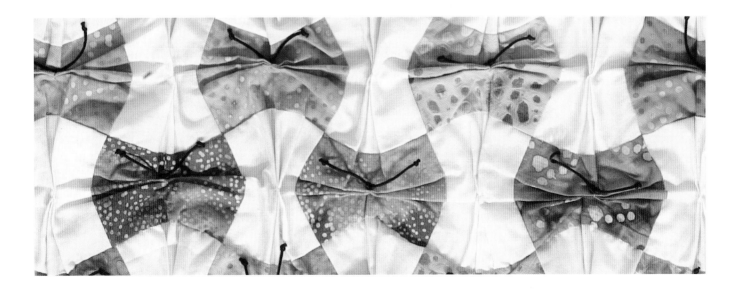

A FRESH TWIST ON FABRIC FOLDING

BUTTERFLY DRESS

Butterfly Dress, Rebecca Wat

ou can incorporate the pleating technique introduced in this chapter into almost any sewing project. To make the little dress shown here, or any dress, just piece all the fabric squares together to achieve the needed size and use it to replace the skirt portion of a commercial pattern of your choice.

MATERIALS

Dress top ¹/₂ yard

Butterflies (skirt) a variety of colorful fabrics to total 1 yard

Decoration ribbon roses or buttons

CUTTING

Dress top Cut the dress top according to your pattern.

Butterflies Cut 60 squares 4″ × 4″.

CONSTRUCTION

1. Arrange the 60 squares into 5 rows of 12.

2. Sew the squares together into rows.

3. Press the seam allowances of each row in alternate directions to make matching the seams easier. Sew the rows together.

4. Assemble the dress top according to your pattern.

5. Sew the skirt portion to the top.

6. Follow the Folding Instructions (page 55) to make pleats.

There are many similarities between the Square Flowers and the Inside-out Flowers. Both are folded flower blocks created from a single piece of fabric, and both are designed to be pieced like a square of fabric. They also both have dimensional petals extending across the boundaries of the square blocks to which they belong. For the Square Flower, none of the petals have any raw edges to tack down. The only sewing you will need to do for a Square Flower block is to piece it just as you would any other fabric square.

FOLDING INSTRUCTIONS

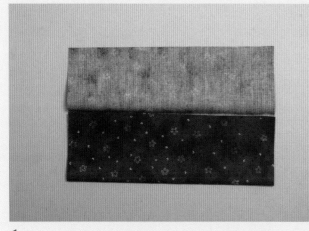

1. Place the fabric wrong side up and fold up one-third of the square. Finger-press to create a crease.

2. Fold down the remaining one-third of fabric. Finger-press to create a crease.

3. Open the fabric square. Rotate the piece 90° and repeat Steps 1 and 2.

4. The creases form 9 squares.

5. Use the creases as a reference to fold 2 adjacent sides inward, creating an ear between them. Finger-press.

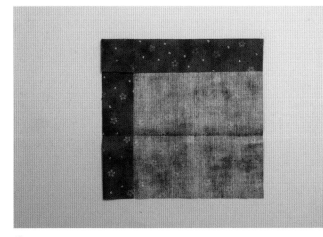

6. Press down the ear to form a square shape. Iron-press.

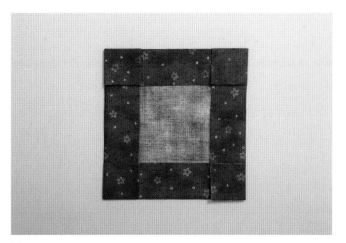

7. Repeat Steps 5 and 6 on the remaining 3 corners.

8. Turn over the fabric.

9. Use the creases as a reference to fold 2 adjacent sides inward, creating an ear between them.

10. Press down the ear to form a square. Iron-press.

11. Repeat Steps 9 and 10 on the remaining corners.

12. Mark the sewing lines.

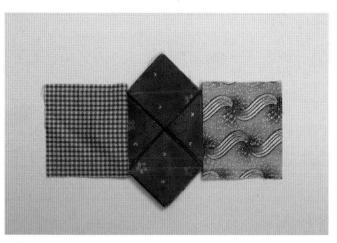

13. Piece the squares to the flower.

14. Piece the strips to the remaining sides of the flower.

15. Open the petals. Iron-press to set. Trim excess fabrics at the back. Tack down the petals if you wish.

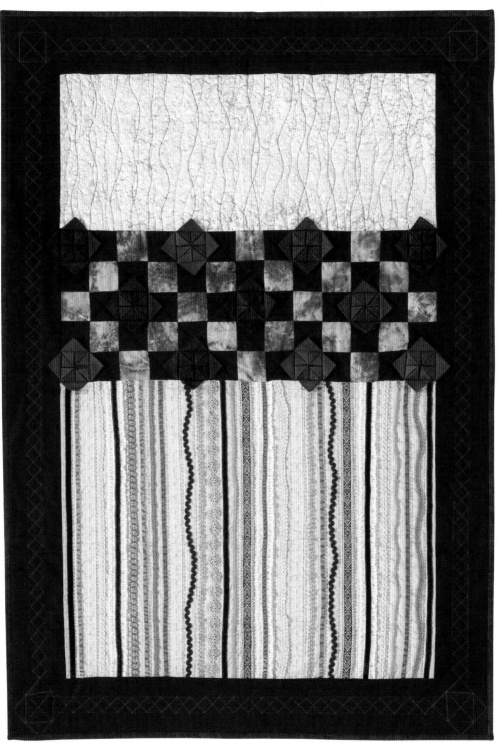

Out of the Square, 35^1/2″ × 52″, **block size: 2″ × 2″, Rebecca Wat**

O *ut of the Square* is a rather abstract design. Lines and squares represent elements like rain, flowers, and leaves, and stems in an unusual way. You need to think outside the box to get it. Ribbons must have been on my mind when I made this quilt, but you may have other ideas.

MATERIALS

Flowers 1 yard

Checkerboard ¹/₂ yard each of a dark and a light fabric

Background 1 yard

Border and binding 1¹/₂ yards

Backing 1⁵/₈ yards

Batting 40″ × 56″

Ribbons and trims A variety of ribbons and trims to total 18 yards (each piece needs to be at least 22″ long)

CUTTING

Flowers Cut 11 squares 9″ × 9″.

Light checkerboard Cut 3 strips 2⁵/₈″ wide × the width of the fabric. Cut strips in half so they are approximately 20″ long.

Dark checkerboard Cut 5 strips 2⁵/₈″ wide × the width of the fabric. Cut strips in half so they are approximately 20″ long.

Background Measure and cut the top and bottom backgrounds during construction (refer to Steps 5–6).

Border Cut 4 strips 4¹/₂″ wide lengthwise.

Binding Cut strips 3¹/₄″ wide lengthwise to total 187″ after piecing the strips end to end (refer to pages 72–74).

FOLDING

Follow the Folding Instructions Steps 1–12 (pages 62–64) to fold the 9″ squares into 11 flowers. Each folded square should measure 3″ × 3″. Do not open the petals until the flowers are pieced to the background.

CONSTRUCTION

1. Sew together 2 light and 3 dark half-strips. Cut into 6 segments 2⁵/₈″ wide.

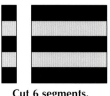

Cut 6 segments.

2. Sew together 1 light and 2 dark half-strips. Cut into 4 segments 2⁵/₈″ wide.

Cut 4 segments.

3. Sew together 1 light and 1 dark half-strip. Cut into 6 segments 2⁵/₈″ wide.

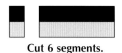

Cut 6 segments.

4. For the center section, arrange and sew the pieces together.

Center Section Construction

5. Measure the exact width of the checkerboard background (it should be approximately 27¹/₂″).

6. Cut the top background fabric to the width from Step 2 × 11″. Cut the bottom background fabric to the same width × 22″.

7. Pin and sew ribbons to the bottom background.

8. Combine the top, center, and bottom background sections.

9. Attach the borders (refer to pages 70–71).

10. Refer to pages 69–74 for quilting and finishing.

BERRY PIE

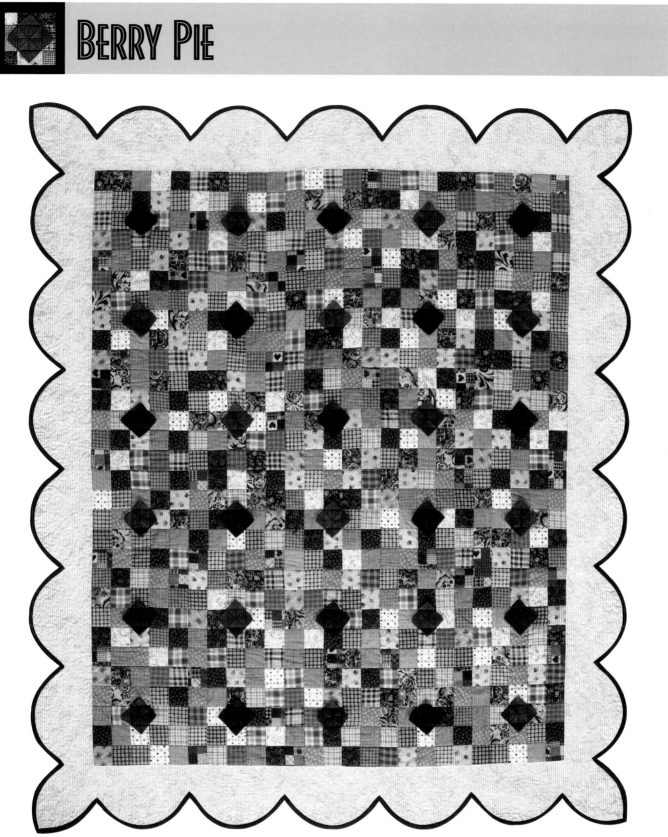

Berry Pie, 68″ × 78³/₄″, **block size: 10⁵/₈″ × 10⁵/₈″, Rebecca Wat, quilted by Julie Murphy**

his is a simple quilt made of square blocks. The pop-up Square Flowers add spice and interest, whereas the almond borders and scalloped edges balance and soften its look. Somehow this quilt makes me think of a fruit pie filled with yummy blueberries, blackberries, raspberries, and strawberries.

MATERIALS

Red flowers 1¼ yards

Navy flowers 1¼ yards

Background 10 or more fabrics to total 5 yards

Border 2½ yards

Binding 1 yard

Backing 4⅝ yards

Batting 72″ × 82″

CUTTING

Red flowers Cut 15 squares 9″ × 9″.

Navy flowers Cut 15 squares 9″ × 9″.

Background Cut strips 2⅝″ wide x the width of the fabric (see Construction below). You will need approximately 48 strips.

Border Cut 4 strips 8″ wide lengthwise.

Binding Cut bias strips 2″ wide to total 370″ (refer to page 73 for continuous bias).

FOLDING

Follow the Folding Instructions (pages 62–64) to fold the 9″ squares into 30 flowers. Each folded square should measure 3″ × 3″. Do not open the petals until you piece the flowers to the background.

CONSTRUCTION

1. Combine and sew 4 strip sets using 2 of the 2⅝″-wide strips. Press. Cut the strip sets into 60 segments 2⅝″ wide.

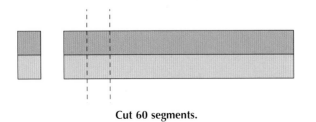

Cut 60 segments.

2. Combine and sew 8 strip sets using 5 of the 2⅝″-wide strips. Press the all the seams in the same direction. Cut the strip sets into 120 segments 2⅝″ wide.

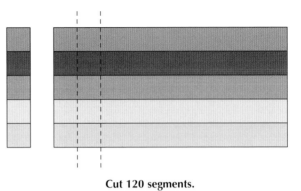

Cut 120 segments.

3. Arrange and sew the pieces together into blocks. Rotate the segments so the seams nest.

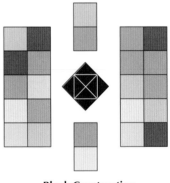

Block Construction

4. Arrange and sew the blocks together into rows of 5 blocks each. Press.

5. Sew the rows together. Press.

6. Attach the borders, and miter the corners (refer to pages 70–71.)

7. Use the templates on pages 77–78 to mark the scalloped border. Do not cut until the quilting is done.

8. Refer to pages 69–74 for quilting and finishing.

9. Refer to page 73 for scalloped binding.

Quilting and Finishing

There are many ways to make a quilt. The methods and techniques that quilters use to construct their quilts vary depending on their background, habits, personal style, and preference. I learned quilting by reading extensively, watching tapes and TV shows, and making frequent visits to local quilt shops, where knowledgeable quilters were available to answer questions and share their opinions and experiences. Another effective way to learn is to attend classes. I encourage you to do all of the above if you love to quilt and want to expand your skills.

This chapter is a brief overview of the quilting process as a reference for beginning quilters. For a few good books on basic quilting, see Resources (page 79).

DESIGN AND PREPARATION

If you'd like to design your own quilt rather than follow specific project instructions, it is helpful to have at least a general idea of the look and size of the quilt you intend to make. Sketch the design on a piece of paper. After refining it, write down the measurements. Finalize the design and draw it to scale on a piece of graph paper. Make a few copies so you can color each copy differently. Before you head to your favorite fabric store, estimate the number of different fabrics you will need and the yardage for each fabric. Once you have assembled all the fabrics, plan a cutting scheme similar to the cutting instructions in this book.

ROTARY CUTTING

A rotary cutter, a cutting mat, and a wide acrylic ruler are essential for efficient and accurate cutting. If you have never used a rotary cutter before, have someone show you the proper way to use it.

Before you cut, press the fabric. Align the fabric with the horizontal markings on the mat, and align the ruler with the vertical markings on the mat. Press down firmly on the ruler with four of your fingertips. Your little finger should be against the outside edge of the ruler, resting on the mat or fabric to keep the ruler from shifting. Hold the cutter with your other hand and cut along the edge of the ruler (the blade of the cutter should rotate during this process). Practice cutting scrap fabrics first. Do not cut the fabrics for your final quilt until you have mastered the skill of rotary cutting. To cut multiple layers of fabric, be sure the folded edges align with the horizontal markings on the mat.

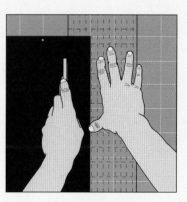

Left-handed cutting

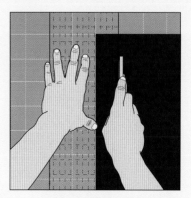

Right-handed cutting

PIECING

You can do piecing either by hand or by machine. Regardless of how you choose to piece, it is important to use a consistent seam allowance. To piece by hand, use a marking tool to draw lines on the wrong side of the fabric $1/4"$ from the raw edges. Place two pieces of fabric right sides together, piece them together with very small running stitches, and end by backstitching.

When piecing by machine, there are several ways to sew $1/4"$ seams:

- Use a $1/4"$ presser foot, which is available for most sewing machines. This type of foot is a good investment if you do a lot of piecing.

- If your machine sews zigzag, you may adjust the needle so that it is $1/4"$ from the edge of the presser foot.

- Find the $1/4"$ mark on the throat plate next to your machine's feed dogs. Place a piece of tape along that mark to extend it as a reference when you sew.

To piece more efficiently, arrange and sew the pieces in pairs, one after another, without cutting the thread or lifting the presser foot. This is called *chain piecing*.

Chain piecing

PRESSING

In general, press seams toward the darker fabric. Press lightly in an up-and-down motion. Avoid using a very hot iron or ironing too much, both of which can distort shapes and blocks. When combining rows, press the seams of one row in the same direction and the seams of the next row in the opposite direction. This allows the seams to nest when you sew the rows together.

APPLIQUÉ

Several of the folded flowers in this book are appliquéd to the background fabric. You can sew appliqués onto the background fabric either by hand or by machine. To hand appliqué, add a turn-under allowance (approximately $1/4"$) when cutting the appliqué shapes. This allowance can be turned under before or after you baste or pin the appliqué onto the background fabric.

To machine appliqué, cut on the drawn lines of the appliqué. Baste or pin the appliqué shapes onto the background fabric before you begin satin stitching (a very close zigzag stitch) with your machine. When satin stitching, be sure the stitches cover the raw edge of the appliqué, not the background fabric, and that all corners and points of the appliqué are well covered.

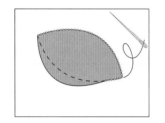

Hand appliqué

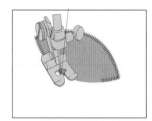

Machine appliqué

BORDERS

In most cases, you will sew on the side borders first. When you have finished the quilt top, measure it through the center vertically. This will be the length to cut the side borders. Place pins at the centers of all four sides of the quilt top, as well as in the center of each side border strip. Pin the side borders to the quilt top, matching the center pins. Use a $1/4"$ seam allowance to sew the borders to the quilt top. Press the seams.

Measure horizontally across the center of the quilt top, including the side borders. This will be the length to cut the top and bottom borders. Repeat pinning, sewing, and pressing as you did for the side borders.

Mitered Corner Borders

Measure the length of the quilt top and add two times the width of your border plus 5˝. This is the length you need to cut or piece for mitered borders.

Place pins at the centers of both side borders and all four sides of the quilt top. From the center pin, measure in both directions and mark half of the measured length of the quilt top on both side borders. Match the centers and the marked length of the side border to the edges of the quilt top and pin. Stitch the strips to the sides of the quilt top. Stop and backstitch at the seam allowance, ¹⁄₄˝ from the edge (see Step 1). The excess length will extend beyond each edge. Press the seams toward the border.

Determine the length needed for the top and bottom border in the same way, measuring the width of the quilt top through the center and including each side border. Add 5˝ to this measurement. Cut or piece these border strips. From the center of each border strip, mark half of the measured width of the quilt top in both directions. Pin, stitch up to the ¹⁄₄˝ seamline, and backstitch. The border strips extend beyond each end.

To create the miter, place the corner on the ironing board. With the quilt right side up, place the top border strip on top of the adjacent side border (see Step 2).

Fold the top border strip under itself so that it meets the edge of the outer border and forms a 45° angle. Press and pin the fold in place (see Step 3).

Position a right-angle triangle or ruler over the corner to check that the corner is flat and square (see Step 4). When everything is in place, press the fold firmly.

Fold the center section of the top diagonally from the corner, right sides together, and align the long edges of the border strips. On the wrong side, place pins near the pressed fold in the corner to secure the border strips.

Beginning at the inside corner, backstitch and stitch along the fold toward the outside point (see Step 5). Be careful not to allow any stretching. Backstitch at the end. Trim the excess border fabric to a ¹⁄₄˝ seam allowance. Press the seam open.

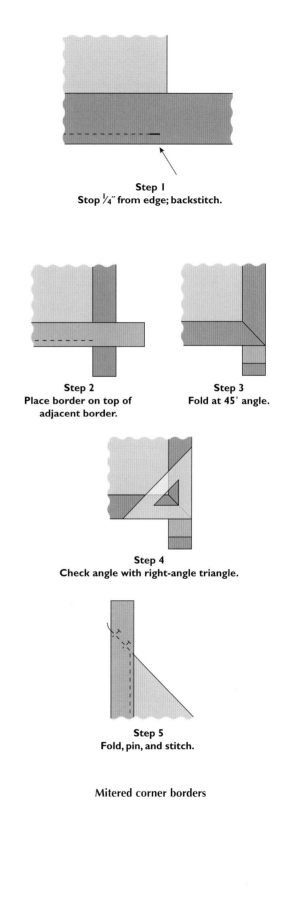

Step 1
Stop ¹⁄₄˝ from edge; backstitch.

Step 2
Place border on top of adjacent border.

Step 3
Fold at 45° angle.

Step 4
Check angle with right-angle triangle.

Step 5
Fold, pin, and stitch.

Mitered corner borders

BACKING

Plan on making the backing a minimum of 2″ larger than the quilt top on all sides. Prewash the fabric and trim the selvages before you piece. To economize, piece the back using any leftover fabrics or blocks in your collection.

BATTING

The type of batting you use is a personal decision; consult your local quilt shop. Cut batting approximately 2″ larger than your quilt top on all sides.

LAYERING

Spread the backing wrong side up and tape down the edges with masking tape. If you are working on carpet, use T-pins to secure the backing to the carpet. Center the batting on top of the backing, smoothing out any folds. Place the quilt top right side up on top of the batting and backing and make sure it is centered.

BASTING

If you plan to machine quilt, pin baste the quilt layers together with safety pins placed a minimum of 3″–4″ apart. Begin basting in the center and move toward the edges first in vertical, then in horizontal, rows.

If you plan to hand quilt, use a long needle and light-colored thread to baste the layers together. Knot one end of the thread. Use stitches approximately the length of the needle. Begin in the center and move out toward the edges.

QUILTING

Quilting, whether by hand or by machine, enhances the quilt's design. You may choose to quilt in-the-ditch, echo the pieced or appliquéd motifs, use patterns from quilting design books and stencils, or do your own free-motion quilting.

BINDING

Double-Fold Straight-Grain Binding (French Fold)

Calculate the length of the binding by adding the measurements of the four sides plus a 12″ allowance. To make a double-fold binding, multiply the desired finished width by 6 and add another $1/4$″. For instance, if you want a $1/2$″ finished binding, cut the strips $3 1/4$″ wide and piece them together with a diagonal seam to make a continuous binding strip.

Press the seams open, then press the entire strip in half lengthwise with wrong sides together. With raw edges even, pin the binding to the edge of the quilt a few inches from the corner. Leave the first few inches of the binding unattached. Start sewing with a $1/2$″ seam allowance.

Stop sewing $1/2$″ from the first corner (see Step 1); backstitch one stitch. Lift the presser foot and needle. Rotate the quilt one-quarter turn. Fold the binding at a right angle so it extends straight above the quilt (see Step 2). Bring the binding strip down even with the edge of the quilt (see Step 3). Begin sewing at the folded edge.

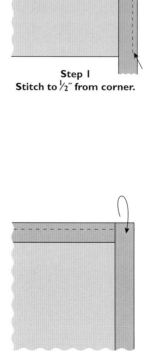

Step 1
Stitch to $1/2$″ from corner.

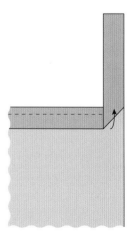

Step 2
Fold up for mitered corner.

Step 3
Fold down.

Continuous Bias Binding

To make continuous bias, you use a square sliced in half diagonally but you sew the triangles together so that you continuously cut the marked strips. Cut the fabric for the bias binding so it is a square. For example, if the yardage is ½ yard, cut an 18″ square. Cut the square in half diagonally to create two triangles.

Use a ¼″ seam allowance to sew these two triangles together. Press the seam open.

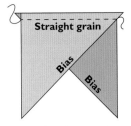

Sew triangles together.

Use a ruler to mark the parallelogram with lines spaced the width you need to cut your bias. Cut along the first line for about 5″.

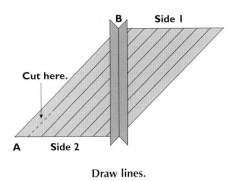

Draw lines.

Join Side 1 and Side 2 to form a tube. Line A will line up with the raw edge at B. This will allow the first line to be offset by one strip width. Pin the raw ends together, making sure that the lines match. Sew with a ¼″ seam allowance. Press seams open. Cut along the marked lines.

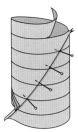

Sew to form tube.

Scalloped Binding

Scalloped quilt edges are bound with bias binding, which is more flexible and conforms better to curves than does straight-grain binding. Bias binding will follow the curves and lie flat.

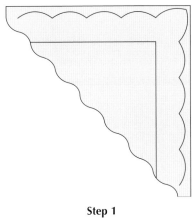

Step 1
Mark design on border.

Use the template patterns on pages 77–78 to mark the scallop design on the border (Step 1). Make bias binding. With the right sides together and the raw edge of the quilt aligned with the raw edge of the bias binding, sew them together with a ½″ seam. Take care not to overstretch the binding as you sew, particularly when you pivot at the pivot point between the curves (Step 2). Turn the binding to the back of the quilt, so it covers the raw edge, and hand stitch the binding to the backing.

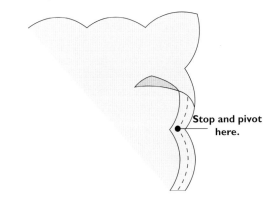

Step 2
Sew binding with 1/2″ seam.

Finishing the Binding

Method 1

Fold under the beginning end of the binding strip ¼″. Place the end binding strip over the beginning folded end. Continue stitching the seam beyond the folded edge. Trim the excess binding. Fold the binding over the raw edges to the quilt back and hand stitch, mitering the corners.

Method 2

Fold the end tail of the binding back on itself where it meets the beginning binding tail. From the fold, measure and mark the cut width of your binding strip. Cut the end binding tail to this measurement. For example, if your binding is cut 3¼″ wide, measure from the fold on the end tail of the binding 3¼″ and cut the binding tail to this length.

Open both tails. Place one tail on top of the other at right angles and with right sides together. Mark a diagonal line and stitch on the line. Trim the seam to ¼″. Press open.

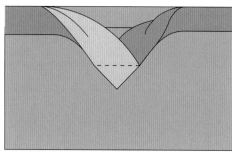

Finishing the binding.

TEMPLATE PATTERNS

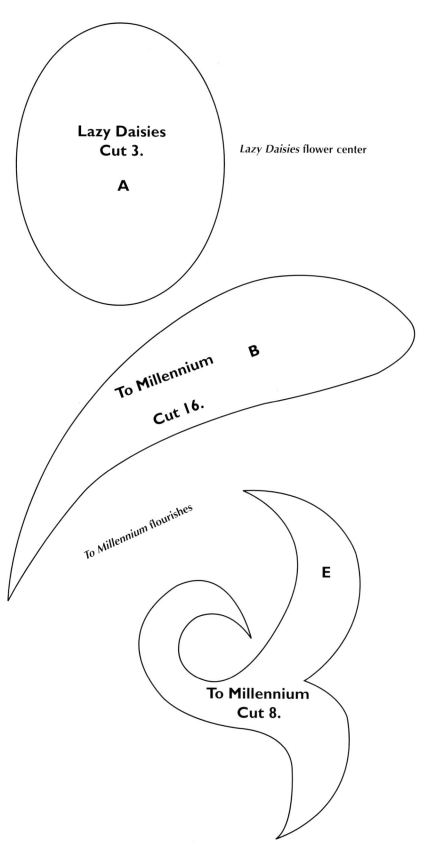

Lazy Daisies
Cut 3.

A

Lazy Daisies flower center

To Millennium
Cut 16.

B

To Millennium flourishes

E

To Millennium
Cut 8.

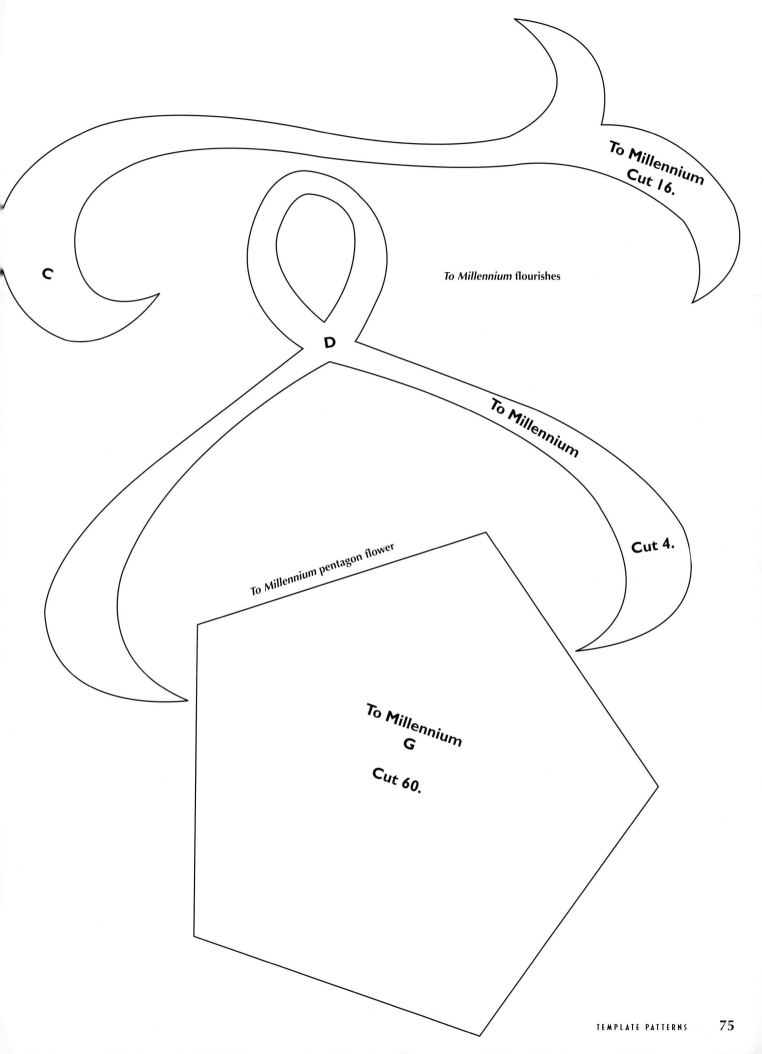

C

To Millennium flourishes

To Millennium
Cut 16.

D

To Millennium

Cut 4.

To Millennium pentagon flower

To Millennium
G

Cut 60.

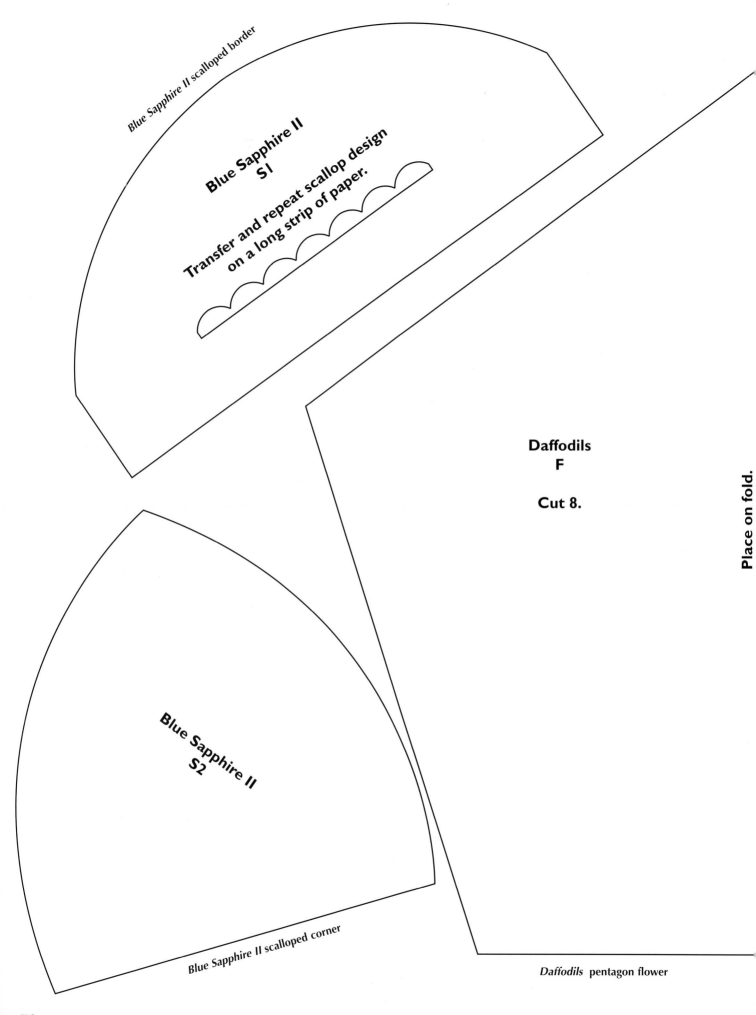

Blue Sapphire II scalloped border

**Blue Sapphire II
SI**

**Transfer and repeat scallop design
on a long strip of paper.**

**Daffodils
F

Cut 8.**

Place on fold.

**Blue Sapphire II
S2**

Blue Sapphire II scalloped corner

Daffodils pentagon flower

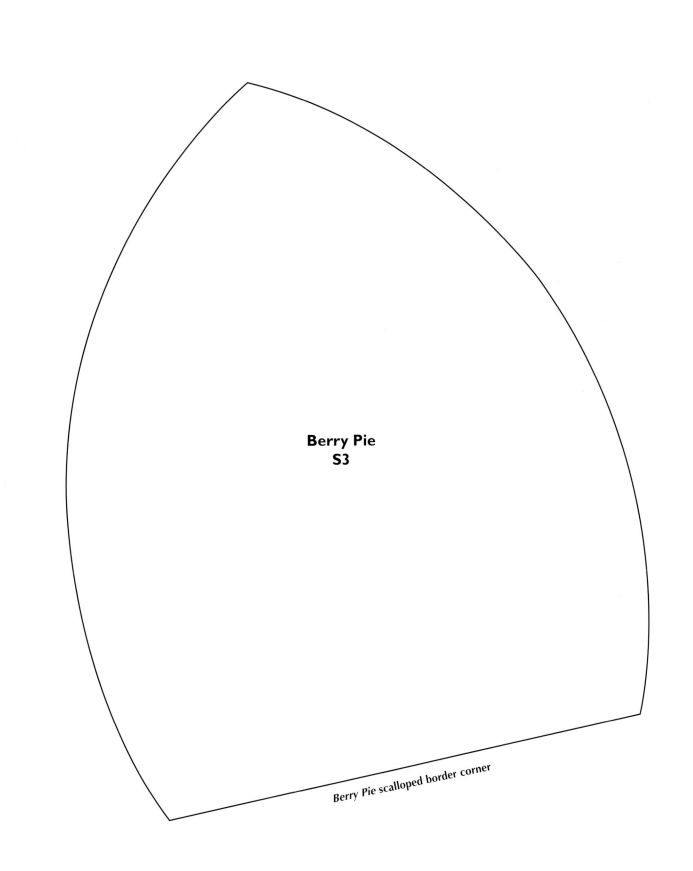

Berry Pie
S3

Berry Pie scalloped border corner

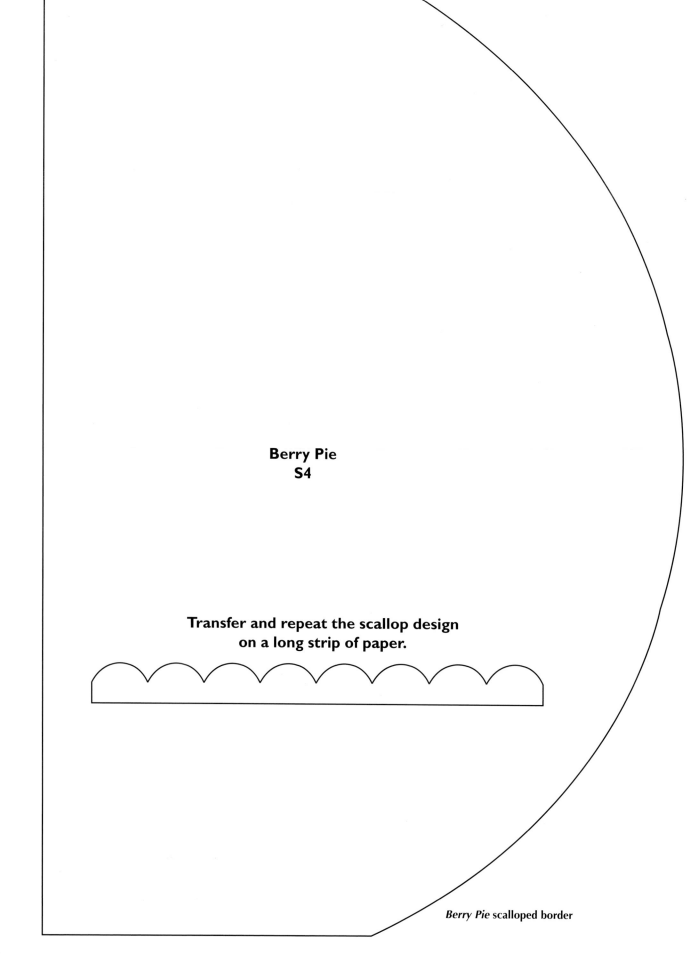

**Berry Pie
S4**

**Transfer and repeat the scallop design
on a long strip of paper.**

Berry Pie scalloped border